Biff the Useless Mention

Biff the Useless Mention

the sequel to 'Sell the Pig', 'Is That Billinge Lump?' and 'Mother Was It Worth It?'

LIVRES
LEMAS

Tottie Limejuice

Published by LEMAS LIVRES
www.tottielimejuice.com

© Copyright L.M.K. Tither 2019
Cover design DMR Creative
Cover photo © Tottie Limejuice

BIFF THE USELESS MENTION

ISBN 978-2-901-77315-3

Contents

To Robin

Stupid Boy!

About the Author

Tottie Limejuice is the pen name of former journalist and freelance copywriter, Lesley Tither. Lesley also writes crime fiction as L M Krier and children's fiction as L M Kay.

Contact Details

If you would like to get in touch, please do so at:

tottielimejuice@gmail.com

facebook.com/LMKrier

facebook.com/groups/1450797141836111/

https://twitter.com/tottielimejuice

http://tottielimejuice.com/

More from the same author

If you've enjoyed this book why not try more from author Lesley Tither under her different pen-names?

Writing travel memoirs/humour as Tottie Limejuice:

> Sell the Pig
> Is That Billinge Lump?
> Mother Was It Worth It?
> Biff the Useless Mention
> Angling Bumateurs
> Maman, vends le cochon
>
> No Girl on This Train
> Hobbit House in Italy

Writing crime fiction as L M Krier:

> The First Time Ever
> Baby's Got Blue Eyes
> Two Little Boys
> When I'm Old and Grey
> Shut Up and Drive
> Only the Lonely
> Wild Thing
> Walk on By
> Preacher Man

Cry for the Bad Man
Every Game You Play
Where the Girls Are

Writing children's fiction as L M Kay:

The Dog with the Golden Eyes

Chapter One
A trilogy of four?

How can you have a fourth book in a trilogy? The *Sell the Pig* series was only ever intended to be a trilogy. But those of you who have read them will know that maths was never my strongest subject.

Despite the best efforts of Mrs Riley Maths (there were two Mrs Rileys at Stockport High School for Girls) I was, and I remain, slightly dyscalculic. I can easily translate figures into various languages, but adding them up and making sense of them defeats me. So, a trilogy of four? Why not!

Eight and a half years have passed since I first crossed the Channel with my elderly, gaga mother and my damaged brother, to start a new life in central France's Auvergne. Well, being pedantic, as ever, we passed under the Channel, rather than over it, aboard the Eurotunnel Shuttle.

After four wonderful years, Mother went to pick blackberries on Billinge Lump for all eternity, her ashes once more laid to rest at Eccleston church, where she was married, in the family plot with her mother and father, eldest sister and a brother.

Sadly, a new start in a new country has not worked the hoped-for miracles with my brother, who continues to lurch from crisis to crisis. There is still no sign of an end to the demons which plague him. He now has social workers trying to keep an eye on him. I'm not sure how much social workers are paid in France, but they are certainly going to earn their wages with his case.

He now has one of those alarm bracelets to summon the *sapeurs-pompiers* (Fire and Rescue Service). He leads them a merry dance. Only the other day the *gendarmes* (police) phoned me to ask his whereabouts. I knew that, it being a Tuesday, he had gone to the English club, the Café Anglais, in Clermont-Ferrand.

It seems my brother had been talking to a new friend he has acquired, saying he was in the depths of despair and needed help. The kind friend had rushed round to the house as soon as he could, but in the meantime my brother had taken himself off into town, without letting anyone know. And so it goes on.

As for me, I am still in love with my adoptive country, all the more so now it has granted me the privilege and honour of becoming French. I love it, warts and all, despite its many little foibles. I love it despite its formidable bureaucracy, which has even the French tearing out their hair.

Well, in the interest of balance, as I write this, there are a few tears of sheer frustration threatening. I find myself, at the time of writing, being in the precarious situation of no longer having the magic '*carte vitale*' (health card) which is the Open Sesame into France's marvellous healthcare system. It took me five years to get one in the first place and now, through no fault of my own, it has been clawed back into the system.

Once again, it's a numbers game which is at the root of my frustration over the past year. And numbers are always my worst nightmare. I've had to battle my way through so many changes in life, because of my age and the way the numbers fall. Things like coping with decimalisation, when Britain changed from the old system of pounds, shilling and pence.

I'd managed to muddle by knowing that there were twelve pennies in a shilling and twenty shillings in a pound. Or was it the other way round? Then I had to adjust to everything being in tens and only having pounds and new pence, as they were called. No more shillings, certainly nary a florin to be found, and perish the thought that the new-fangled decimalisation should include anything as exotic as a half-crown.

More changes later on, with the changeover to metric measurements from Imperial. I never did quite get my head round that, so I arrived in France not having a clue what my five feet four inches was in metres, nor what nine stone amounted to in kilogrammes.

I was born in 1952, which means that I fall into the Twilight Zone, caught up in the restructuring of the retirement age for women from sixty to sixty-five. I became entitled to draw a pension from the UK once I reached sixty-two years and four months, so I decided to grab it quickly with both hands and to retire from my job as a freelance copywriter.

It was increasingly getting hard to summon and maintain enthusiasm for my job. Technology is constantly evolving, of course, and an old dinosaur like me was always lagging behind knowing how to use wondrous new inventions. It didn't help having an Internet connection which was as slow as a slow thing on national go-slow day. Truly a piece of wet string, as my good friend Alex, a computer systems analyst, was always saying, between curses, when he came to stay and had to adapt to being away from his ultra-fast fibre optic speeds.

It should be plain sailing, taking my retirement in both countries. I had never worked on the black in my life, had always paid all my contributions in both the UK and France. I was entitled to a full UK pension and a tiny one from my French contributions, which would at least prove that I had paid into the system.

Plain sailing? Who was I kidding? This is me we're talking about!

It wasn't just technological advances which meant I'd grown tired of my work as a copywriter. I found the writing, too, was getting harder, the older I got. Especially living out here in the sticks of my beloved Auvergne. I'd never been truly

3

interested in the latest fashions, although I'd written about them for long enough.

But here, where people, although well turned-out, opt for casual in even the smartest of restaurants, it was getting harder to wax lyrical about expensive gowns and party frocks which couldn't even be washed or dry-cleaned. What's that all about? In my days of working in Further Education, I used to lecture on sustainable development and in-built obsolescence, so the very idea goes against the grain for me.

Working as a copywriter in the UK, I had managed to keep up online with the latest fashions, even though they had never greatly interested me. Here, sitting at my desk with the door open to the garden and the fields beyond, I was far more interested in the marvels of nature outside. The familiar sound of a returning migratory bird would have me abandoning my keyboard and rushing outside to listen to old friends coming home.

The cuckoo was always the first of the migrants to start shouting his presence, either late March or early April, followed in succession by the swallows around the middle of the month, then the hoopoes and last, the brightly coloured golden orioles with their fluting, melodic song. The colours of these birds, especially the males in their courting plumage, interested me far more than who was wearing what frock for the latest red carpet occasion.

Time to call a halt and stop doing it, then. Early retirement would mean I was living on buttons for the rest of my life, but I didn't mind that. There would be my UK old age pension, and my infinitesimal one in France. I also had a tiny personal pension, plus the royalties from my various book sales. It wouldn't amount to much, but my material wants have always been small. I genuinely don't know what I would do if ever I came into a lot of money, apart from see my friends right and buy a big field for the dogs to play in.

Retirement would also mean that, instead of spending hours

at the computer, bashing out work for ever-more demanding clients, struggling to meet increasingly impossible deadlines, I would have more time for doing all the things which I love. Gardening, discovering the area I now live in, walking and training my dogs, enjoying camping trips with them and catching up with friends over coffee, or long, leisurely lunches.

'Be Prepared', said that nice Lord Baden-Powell, of Scouting fame, and I always am, having been a Brownie, then a Tawny Owl and a Guide Lieutenant. I started filling in all the necessary forms in plenty of time for my planned retirement date in July 2014. And that, in France, involved a lot of '*biffer la mention inutile*'.

This splendid phrase is one of several used here for 'delete where not applicable.' Translated literally, it means 'biff the useless mention'. I had to do a lot of biffing, as I waded through a succession of forms for both the UK and the French authorities, which all contained lots of useless mentions.

French bureaucracy is legendary. Even the French are in awe of it. But it has to be said, some of my problems started on the other side of the Channel, back in dear old Blighty.

To be sure I had all the correct forms to wave at their counterparts here, I first contacted the Department of Work and Pensions in Britain. In fact, I spoke to them three times at least, as what I was told each time, which was always different, didn't accord with what already-retired friends here were telling me.

And if anyone knows of a more expensive way to listen to Vivaldi than being stuck on hold to the DWP in the UK, do please let me know.

After that, things went so pear-shaped it would take up most of this book to tell you about it. Which would be boring in the extreme. All you need to know for now is that, between hitches and delays by the DWP and two bodies here in France, RAM and CIPAV, I currently find myself without a health card and not yet in possession of my titchy French pension.

I am, in effect, status-less. I'm no longer working, so no longer paying any contributions, so I no longer count as self-employed. But I can't prove my status as an officially retired person here in France, as the CIPAV, after fourteen months of requests, have still not produced the necessary form for me to do so.

In the meantime, that nice Mr Cameron, in his wisdom, has been busily washing his hands on the quiet of older people who dare to slope off to live in another country. He's already said we can't have the winter fuel payments which were previously our rights because France is a warm country. I am tempted to show him the yard-long icicle which routinely appears from the down-spout of my barn roof every winter. And not by putting it in front of his eyes, either.

He's also decreed that if we have ever paid into the system in our adoptive countries in Europe, we are no longer entitled to the magic S1 form, proving us to be pensioners. Fair enough. But nobody has told the French, so they keep asking me for it and won't resolve my situation without one.

Think of it as an international tennis match, with me as the ball. The current situation is that the umpire has given a line fault and called for new balls.

Perhaps, as this book unfolds, I'll be able to update you with news of a breakthrough on the bureaucracy front. In the meantime, I dare hardly venture out, being without my health card. As I get older and increasingly accident prone, I fear the prospect of an incident involving costly medical bills, without the means to pay them.

However, the eternal optimist, as ever, I continue to sally forth into battle to try to find a way forward, and in particular, to get my paws on my little bit of a top-up pension. Because, in order to make ends meet, I've had to take to a life of crime. But more of that anon.

What you really want to know first is about life in the rural Auvergne. Am I right? You want to catch up with all your favourite characters, like the Bowing Farmer, and Kevin the Kitchen Range. To find out what's been happening to them all, and perhaps to meet some new ones. To discover if the grottage ever got finished, or if I'm even still living there.

So, are you ready to join me for more Tottie's Tours of the Livradois-Forez? But, in typical Tottie style, let's begin by putting the kettle on and dishing up the cake.

Earl Grey, anyone?

Chapter Two
Sell the Cochon

The first thing French people ask me, when I tell them that I'm a writer, is have my various books been translated into French yet, especially the *Sell the Pig* series. That's because they are all dying to know why I left England to set up home in France, and particularly in the Auvergne.

For some reason, most of the French people I encounter have a vision of the UK as a real land of milk and golden honey. They have visions of almost full employment, affordable housing for all, and, of course, the wonderful free health service.

Just for fun one time, for a class of English learners I was teaching, I brought in some estate agents' details. It was a bit mischievous of me to pick Alderley Edge, where the prices are hugely elevated because the Beckhams kept a home there. I chose a fairly modest gentleman's residence, five bedrooms, detached, but really nothing to get all that excited about.

I told them it was in a well-heeled part of the country, comparing it to the wealthier outskirts of our regional capital city, Clermont-Ferrand, such as Royat, which is about as pricey as it gets round here. Their guesses were all around the three hundred and fifty thousand Euro bracket. They took some convincing when I revealed the actual asking price to be five million pounds sterling.

Because the *Sell the Pig* books explain a bit more about the reality, and in particular, give the answer to why I chose the Auvergne above any other region of France, I decided that a translation would be a great idea. Then when people asked, I could just point them at the French version. More sales for me, all their questions answered. Perfect!

I know that good translators don't come cheap. I had already been looking round and the prices quoted were eye-watering, way beyond my humble means as a mere Indie – an independently published writer. But I thought I'd keep on asking about, to see if I could find someone within my price range.

I hasten to say at the outset, that to avoid any lawsuit for defamation, I am not going to mention anything at all to identify the person I engaged, not even their gender, nor where they came from. Henceforth, they will be referred to only as That Person, or TP for short. Although, between friends, I refer to TP as something rather less polite than that.

My first conversation with TP was encouraging. They certainly had a good mastery of English. Although I should perhaps have been more wary of the fact that they insisted on demonstrating that to me by keeping up a long monologue, not allowing me to get much of a word in edgeways.

TP also barely asked about the book which was to be translated to start with, *Sell the Pig* itself. That was the first in what was previously a trilogy and has now morphed into a series of four. But TP had lived 'oop north' in England. Not in Stockport where I grew up, nor yet in Lancashire, the source of many of Mother's funny little sayings. But they should, in all probability, manage with some of the northern slang and sayings. And of course I, the writer, was never more than an email away for clarification.

Nothing could possibly go wrong. Surely?

One of the hardest things to translate accurately was always going to be Mother's favourite saying, the one which gave rise to the title of the series.

'Mother, mother, it's a bugger, sell the pig and buy me out,' is said to have been a telegram home from a disgruntled conscript not enjoying his first taste of army life. Family legend claims it was some distant great-uncle of mine who originated it, but I think many other families also make the same claim.

Wherever it came from, it's a tricky one to translate. That's because only those from that area of England, or from south Wales, would be likely to know that in this case, 'bugger' has nothing whatever to do with its usual, literal, meaning. It simply means, in the context, adverse circumstances, hard times. Ironically, the origin of the word is old French, *bougre,* meaning heretic, and is nowadays quite a mild expression, with none of the *double-entendre* of the English word.

Unfortunately, TP chose a phrase not dissimilar to 'a load of bollocks' with which to translate bugger in the saying, when they produced the first few pages for approval. Now, my mother would say bugger, as it's not at all uncommon in Lancashire, where she was born. Even then she would half-whisper the word, aware that it could sound wrong. But my mother saying bollocks? Never in a million years! I suspect she may never even have heard the word. She had led a relatively sheltered life.

With my usual optimism, though, I waited for TP to produce more of my work translated into French, hoping we could work through any early disagreements on buggers and bollocks. And, apart from those and a few other expressions which didn't quite sit right with me, I was, overall, pleased with the initial effort, a translation of the first chapter. So I instructed TP to continue, expecting to get the rest of it a chapter or two at a time.

To me, the first pass sounded exactly as I would say it myself it if I were to try to explain the book in my halting French to French friends. In that sense, it appeared to have captured my voice. Once again, I missed the warning signs.

SELL THE COCHON

I was quite surprised that TP didn't contact me very much at all to check on obscure meanings. I had fully expected to have to rewrite a few passages, so they would make more sense to a French readership. But no, TP was whizzing through it with almost indecent haste, informing me that they were eager to get it finished. They made it sound like a chore. Not exactly flattering, to an author.

In the meantime, I had handed TP's trial efforts to my trusty team of French beta readers. They are those essential 'second eyes' who read through a writer's work, often before the editing stage, to point out any howlers where something makes no sense. Importantly, my team included some friends who had known my mother, so would know absolutely if the translation faithfully captured both my, and my mother's, tone of voice.

Their verdict was unanimous, and disappointing. TP's efforts read as if someone armed with a dictionary had sat down and translated my original work word by word, losing all of the feeling of the original. They were all in agreement about 'bollocks', too. None of them could visualise such a strong word coming from the mouth of my dear old white-haired mother, even at her worst behaved.

Then came the full, supposedly finished 'don't find too many errors' version from TP, together with their invoice. And yes, that was actually the comment from TP, who didn't seem to think it was in any way their job to put right any errors which may have occurred.

In some ways, it put me in mind of Pedro Carolino's famous 19th century Portuguese-English phrase-book, relaunched as 'English As She Is Spoke'. That book was an attempt at translation by someone who apparently couldn't the grasp the true meaning of words, even if they managed to find their literal meaning. This gave rise to such unforgettable phrases as 'to craunch a marmoset' and, under the apt heading of 'Idiotisms and proverbs', the wonderful 'Nothing some money, nothing of Swiss.'

TP's rendition of *Sell the Pig* was accurate enough, in its own way. But the interpretation of some of the words and phrases, carefully explained in long, verbose foot-notes, actually did have me laughing to the point of incontinence.

You may remember the foul-tempered family cat, mentioned earlier in the *Sell the Pig* trilogy of four? Topsy, named after the slave girl in Uncle Tom's Cabin, because she 'just growed' and she certainly was wicked. She had somehow morphed into a rogue elephant at a tourist attraction who had been publicly put to death. In other words, TP appeared simply to have applied the first Google reference to Topsy they had found, without checking with me that it was the right one.

My personal favourite concerned our poor French teacher at school, a certain Mrs Twitchett. My fellow pupils and I all thought her name very apt as we behaved so badly in her class that we soon had her twitching with nerves. She was too nice to be in charge of a class of thirty-one monstrous young girls.

TP had clearly once again simply Googled the word Twitchett and come up with an Urban Dictionary definition as a southern slang word for the vagina. Now that may well be so, but that is definitely southern slang from the United States, not Great Britain, and seemingly quite obscure at that.

I can assure you that boater-wearing, gym-slipped eleven-year-old pupils of Cheshire's Stockport High School for Gels, as our headmistress, Miss Humphries-Edwards, insisted on calling it, had probably never heard of a vagina, never mind a twitchet. I suspect it's much more modern slang anyway than 1963 when I first started at the school.

Poor Mrs Vagina will never see the light of the day. I had to tell TP that I could not possibly use any of their translation. It was just so far off the mark and our efforts to work on it together to get it right had been unsuccessful. We spent nearly three hours arguing on the difference between a caravan and a camping car, for example, as they had used the incorrect French term. It was simply never going to work.

But now I am working with another translator who seems to be at least as mad as I am, so we should be able to get along. We first met through Facebook, and have met up in the flesh a few times. It helps that she understands the English idioms and particularly that she has the gumption to ask where a meaning is unclear.

Apart from me telling her about Mrs Vagina and Topsy the Killer Elephant, she has not had sight of TP's abomination and is coming at the project with fresh eyes. I even took the opportunity to edit the original manuscript to make it perhaps a little easier to translate for the French market.

Soon, hopefully, my French neighbours will be able to find out all about the strange, exotic old hippy who now dwells amongst them. Though I may well have to tone down some of my descriptions of the French, and of the locals in particular, in the interests of the *entente cordiale*.

Chapter Three
Worth It?

It was quickly approaching the third anniversary of when my mother died, four days after her ninety-fourth birthday, a date which also fell close to the UK date for Mothers' Day. For the first two years' mind dates, I'd been away on a trip of reflection and contemplation. For a variety of reasons, I'd decided that, after the third, I wouldn't continue to do the same thing, but would pass the time in some other way.

To mark the occasion of the third anniversary, I decided to go abroad. Not exactly, but at least to venture into the neighbouring Rhône-Alpes region. We were soon to become part of the same vast super-region, because of local government reorganisation. So it was time I went to have a look over the other side of the Forez mountains at what our neighbours had to offer. I'd only briefly crossed over the regional border to the east once before.

It was always hard finding somewhere to camp out of season. Mother's birthday was the twenty-eighth of March and few camp-sites here are open at that time of year. I'd probably already visited all those which were and I wanted to see different sights, to have a bit of an adventure. Hence the need to explore outside the Auvergne. Well, at least a few kilometres over the dividing line.

Alex and I had already ventured into the Loire *département* of the Rhône-Alpes region on one occasion, to visit a museum of the twentieth century, for its fascinating exhibition on the Second World War. The area was picturesque and not too far to drive, so I started trawling the Internet for anything around there with year-round camping and some points of interest.

I like different, quirky, original, especially when choosing a venue for my mini-breaks. When I saw a farm which advertised, amongst its various types of accommodation, ChaletRavanes, my interest was piqued. From the photos, it seemed that a ChaletRavane was a caravan with a large chalet-type extension built onto the side of it.

My normal choice is to camp in one of my collection of tents – I have four to choose from – but these mini-breaks were special occasions when I liked to push the boat out and afford myself a little luxury.

Best of all, the site was open all year, every day, according to its website, and was on an organic farm, with plenty to see and do in the area. It sounded perfect!

For once, I didn't want wifi. I had recently finished writing Book III in the *Sell the Pig* trilogy of four, *Mother, Was It Worth It?* I needed peace and quiet to do the editing. The Internet is a wonderful place, but it's also a wicked time-waster.

I love hearing from friends and readers all round the world. Social media is fantastic for keeping in touch and making new friends. It's not just an empty gesture, me putting my contact details in my books, as I do love to get feedback. But sometimes, when you need to work, it's good to go without Internet access, especially as I'm incapable of ignoring it when it's there in front of me.

Back in my childhood I loved having pen-friends, and social media is much the same, only instantaneous. Well, apart from the different time zones. Growing up, I wrote to Mary Muradzikwa in what was then Rhodesia, to Albert in Malaysia and to various pen-pals in France, Régine, Mireille, Martine. It cost me a fortune in stamps! At least social media is free, but it is seriously addictive. So a ChaletRavane on an organic farm in the Forez, out of season, without wi-fi, sounded the ideal writers' retreat.

I would often leave the cats in the barn with plenty of food and water for a couple of nights when I went away camping. But for a slightly longer trip away, I wanted someone to keep an eye on them, to be sure they were all right. Time to call on those wonderful cat-whisperers, my good friends Tom and Chrissie.

We first met on Facebook and became good virtual friends before meeting up for the first time on one of Jill's visits, when she and I were staying in a brightly-painted hippy chalet in the Cantal *département*. That's where Tom and Chrissie have their 'house-which-can-never-be-a-home,' so it wasn't far for them to come over to see us.

Theirs is a long and complicated story, one I've touched on previously, so I won't go into great detail here. Just to recap, they bought a house, having done everything by the book. Unfortunately, they'd come up against estate agents and lawyers who were, at best, economical with the truth. They discovered their new house came with two added extras that were not mentioned, in the form of sitting tenants who were almost impossible to dislodge.

Tom and Chrissie had to take to the road, wandering around as 'Hobos in France', sometimes house- or animal-sitting, sometimes having to live in a tent. Their enforced lifestyle took a dreadful toll on the health of them both, yet I have never met a couple less prone to complain about their lot than they are.

They had experience of sitting different animals, but I knew cats were their first love. I felt confident they would be able to cope even with the demands of HRH la Princesse Freddie Mercury, my little half-Siamese pussy cat. Her sidekick, Bibi, is the easiest, most biddable and purriest cat imaginable, no trouble to anyone.

But HRH is, as the French say, '*un peu special*'. In the past, when I've had friends call in to check on the cats, they've never even seen her and often start to doubt her existence. She's not keen on strangers, and with a few dozen boxes and beds in the large barn in which to hide, she's sometimes harder to spot than Bigfoot. I felt sure even she might be tempted to venture out and show herself for my friends, the champion cat-sitters.

I was going away for a long weekend, leaving on the Thursday afternoon, once Tom and Chrissie had arrived and settled in, returning on the Monday, late morning. My journey would not be long as I was not actually going far in actual miles, or kilometres, although it felt like quite an adventure, passing outside the boundaries of the Auvergne.

The route took me over the Forez mountains, further south than my usual crossing point of Col du Béal, via the Col des Supeyres, a first for me. This early in the year, there was still some snow on the ground up there. Much to my delight, the first thing I saw at the summit was a hovering short-toed eagle, no doubt just back from his winter migration. My favourite raptor of them all! I took it as a good omen for a successful trip.

I drove a bit further, until we were below the snowline, then stopped for a walk with the dogs. It's always a relief to get Fleur out of the van so she stops barking for a minute! Then we were on our way to find our ChaletRavane, with another brief stop on the way, unscheduled, this time.

I love birds, and everything to do with them. Not in an obsessive, twitcher sort of way. I'm not particularly knowledgeable, but I do take an interest. The longer I live in my rural idyll, the more I mark the passing seasons by the departure and return of migrating birds, rather than by the actual calendar date. So when I came to a viewpoint with a large information board listing bird species, I had to stop for a look.

The place was called the Col de Baracuchet and is apparently one of the best, though not the most prestigious, sites from which to watch migrating birds in autumn. According to the information on the board, they apparently fly only a few metres above the heads of the watchers. I made a mental note to return for a closer look at the right time of year.

I found the farm with no difficulty, parked the van and left the dogs in it while I went to find someone to tell me which was my appointed ChaletRavane. Just as well I left them as I was greeted first by a large, bouncy, but friendly St Bernard dog. My two would have kicked off at the mere sight of her.

My ChaletRavane was impressive. Well, the chalet part was. The Ravane was just an old caravan, nothing exciting, and decidedly cold. The wooden structure, the Chalet part, had a mini-kitchen area with gas hob, microwave and coffee-maker. Kettles are a rarity in France, since people drink more coffee than tea. Also tea here is seldom made with boiling water, it's hot at best but more often not even that.

There was a dining table and chairs, which would make an excellent work-station for my editing, electric heating and what looked to be a comfortable *clic-clac*, or bed-settee. Even with no heating on, it was much warmer in the wooden chalet part than in the old caravan. I knew where I'd be sleeping.

There was just one small snag which had not been clear from the photos and description on the website. My ChaletRavane had no running water. Nothing in which to wash, either me or the dishes, and no loo. Not such a big deal, as a bit of exploring revealed a clean loo and shower block just down the hill nearer to the reception. It would still be a chilly trot if I needed to go in the night.

Most of the space in the sanitary block was taken up with an impressive collection of geraniums, clearly having over-wintered well and getting ready to go back outside at the first rise in temperatures. Or are we meant to call them zonal pelargoniums now? I get confused at the horticultural name changes – it must be a sign of advancing age. Even more confused when the automatic spell-checker offered to call them 'pandemoniums' for me.

The dogs and I settled into a nice relaxed routine for our time away. After a quick morning walk around the camp-site perimeter for the dogs' benefit, and breakfast for all of us, I'd pack up a picnic lunch and a flask for tea and we'd go off exploring.

One of our first trips out was back to the bird migration site, where I'd spotted a signed trail which started from there, which looked like a nice walk. There was a holder on the big sign which should have had route maps of the trail but which was empty. A notice nearby told me that if it was empty, maps were available from the village shop, a mere five kilometre walk away.

Not far, and a nice walk, by the look of it. But then the trail started at the noticeboard, where I was standing, and appeared to go off in a different direction to where the village was, so I would be clocking up ten kilometres before I had even begun the walk. I decided just to explore, without the benefit of a map. After all, I couldn't get lost, with two trusty collie dogs to find the way.

Ci in particular was always an excellent trail-finder. I liked to tease him on walks by asking him to find the van, when I actually knew where it was as I had the map. He would always give me his anguished, 'oh no, you've not lost it again, have you?' look, but invariably found it for me. Fleur was far too much the dizzy blonde and was just as likely to take me off hunting rabbits or deer than bother to look for the van.

We had some brilliant walks. I can read a map well enough but sometimes don't quite appreciate how steep a route is until I find myself struggling up and down formidable hills. Somehow, we always emerge unscathed. Although I did notice that lately Ci was getting a bit reluctant to jump back into the van after some of the longer walks. I assumed that, like me, he was starting to get a few twinges of arthritis which were making themselves felt after a bit of vigorous exercise. I knew how he felt.

One thing we found out about the Loire, on the eastern side of the Forez mountains, was the strength of the wind. Although it was not particularly cold, it seemed to howl away like a banshee most of the time we were there. I managed to get my leg trapped in the van door slamming shut a couple of times. I'd be trying to take picnic stuff out and get caught by a sudden violent gust. The dogs constantly had their ears and fur blown about all over the place. I don't know if it's always like that or was just freak weather, but it was noticeably windier than over on our side of the mountains.

In between the walks, I beavered away on *Mother, Was It Worth It?* or MWIWI as I had affectionately dubbed it prior to publication. I'm incredibly superstitious and never like to reveal the title of a new book until it's ready for pre-order, so they all have code-names or initials.

Without the constant temptations and distractions of the Internet, I made huge strides which would have taken me far longer at home. Despite my best resolve, at home I would have no doubt kept dipping into Facebook and Twitter every few minutes. Just to catch up, as I always told myself.

I treated myself to a nice lunch out on one day of my visit. When I was looking around for a restaurant, quite by chance I found the same *auberge* (inn) which Alex and I had stopped at one our way to the museum, and I hadn't even realised I was in exactly the same area.

We'd both been impressed on that occasion by the enormous portions, great quality and very reasonable prices. I seemed to get a bowl of vegetables, all to myself, of at least the same size as that which the two of us had shared. The chef was an elderly-looking woman who seemed to be coping effortlessly with covers for several dozen people. The dining room was packed, as it had been on our last visit.

It was traditional in style, with long trestle tables, so you could find yourself sharing with complete strangers, which was always good fun. I'd mentioned my Silly Coeliac and Madame herself trotted out of the kitchen a couple of times to make sure she wasn't about to give me the wrong thing. I felt I needed to ask for a wheelbarrow in which to wheel my disgustingly full stomach back to the van after I'd finished eating.

There was another unexpected culinary treat just up the road awaiting me, although it was sheer gluttony which allowed me to indulge. Driving back to the camp-site, I spotted a sign for honey, and honey is one of my most favourite things. I could give Winnie the Pooh, Yogi Bear or anyone else a run for their money in the honey stakes.

This was all locally produced honey and, best of all, you could taste before you bought. I had thought I couldn't possibly eat another morsel until the following morning at least after my enormous lunch. I must have managed to taste a good dozen or so different honeys, though, before making my final selection. One was wickedly dark, from evergreen tree pollen, the other light, clear and fragrant, from the flowers of the high mountain pastures. I could happily have bought up half the shop.

One evening I booked a meal in the farmhouse, just to be sociable. It was just me, two other visitors and the woman and her two daughters who ran the farm and the camping. I'd explained to them about the Silly Coeliac and the need for extreme vigilance, which gave me the perfect excuse not to eat the salami-style *saucisson* which was the starter, as they couldn't guarantee that it was gluten free.

The next course was a wonderful vegetable soup, so thick you could easily have trotted several mice across it, with the farmyard cat in hot pursuit. It was delicious. There was no choice of food, it was dish of the day or nothing. The main course was goat and although I'm not a vegetarian, I always try to avoid eating mammals. But my hosts had already gone to a lot of trouble to accommodate my enforced dietary requirements. I felt that I couldn't really raise any objections on the grounds of lifestyle choice, rather than necessity. It was a farm, after all. So I managed to eat a slice, secure in the knowledge that the kid would have had a good life on the farm.

Nobody spoke any English and I neither asked nor expected them to. It was a nice opportunity to meet some new people and chat to them about the cultural differences between the French and the English, always a lively topic for debate.

My short break was soon over. Time to pack up the van once more, leave the cosy ChaletRavane and head back over the Col to relieve Tom and Chrissie of cat-sitting duties. Chrissie had got on splendidly with HRH, even being allowed to stroke the royal fur. Tom, on the other hand, had been decreed a dangerous potential assassin for daring to cough in the royal presence. Siamese genes, eh? It takes more than fifty per cent moggy ones to cancel them out!

Chapter Four
Aux Armes, Citoyens!

I'm not sure if I actually expected to feel totally different once I had officially become a French person. If I'd hoped suddenly to wake up speaking fluent French, those hopes were dashed. I now get by in almost all circumstances, but I still make some wonderful mistakes. I've never minded laughing at myself, though, and have never yet got myself into a really awkward situation by using the wrong word.

One of my recent howlers had my neighbour looking at me as if she now had categoric proof that '*ils sont fous ces anglais*', 'they're mad, these English', to paraphrase Astérix. '*Rouquin*' is a word for a red-headed person, and is used here often for ginger cats. '*Requin*', on the other hand, is a shark. I'll leave your imagination to fill in the blanks when the mad English hippy woman assured her French neighbour solemnly that she'd had a stray shark in the garden that same day.

Sometimes it's simply that my enthusiasm, and my mouth, run away too fast for what I laughingly call my brain. Hence the bewildered look of French friends when, in a discussion of big brands *versus* supermarkets' own, I told them with great authority that on a recent blind taste test in London, even professional mesh-sprung bed bases could not tell the difference between various bottles of champagne. No, Tottie, you silly tart. *Sommelier* is the word for wine waiter. *Sommier* is the bed base.

One big advantage of acquiring French citizenship was that it meant I got a French passport and a French ID card, which every French person has to carry at all times. And this meant I might finally stop having to pay thirty per cent tax on every book I sell in the United States.

Unlike most other countries, for some reason, Uncle Sam insists on being sent an original document to prove identity, preferably a passport. As a British citizen in France, I only had my British passport, which the law required me to carry always. I was not at that stage entitled to an ID card, so I could not send that. Most countries will accept a photocopy signed by a *notaire,* solicitor, as proof of identity. Not our cousins over the water, it seems.

By sending them my British passport, I was finally able to be issued with the ITIN, individual taxpayer's identification number, so my tax withholding in the US went from thirty per cent to zero. Now all I have to do is to find a way to recuperate all the tax I had already paid as I've not managed to get any response at all from the tax office, either by phone or by letter, as to how to do so.

When I first embarked on the steps necessary to change nationality, a lot of Brits were asking me why I was bothering. But here we are, in 2015, with increasing noises being made about a Brexit, a British exit from the European Union. Suddenly, people on Facebook and Twitter are starting to panic about the possible implications, and asking me how they, too, can become French citizens. I'm trying not to smirk.

First step for morphing into a fully-fledged French person was to go and get a French passport from the *mairie* (town hall) in nearby Ambert, my administrative centre for such things. Ambert boasts a splendid circular building, with archways over a covered walk-way, which used to be the *mairie.* The modern replacement is much less interesting, but fully functional. At least the beautiful old building is still there and hosts a vibrant market every Thursday.

At the *mairie* they would issue my new passport, which they did swiftly and efficiently, although of course there was the usual stack of forms to fill in, with the usual *inutiles mentions* to be biffed. My own local *mairie* furnished me with a French ID card, again after much form-filling, but also quite swiftly. Being a French person was already proving to have some advantages.

With my now redundant British passport on its way to the States for a hopefully brief visit, I could keep my nice, shiny new French one to wave at anyone who wanted me to prove my identity. That meant, in turn, that when people asked if I was English, I could reply triumphantly that I was as French as they were.

But, although I now had all the necessary paperwork, I had not been formally welcomed as a new 'Frog' in an official ceremony. The one planned for earlier in the year, which I should have attended, had been postponed as there were not enough of us being 'frogified' at the same time to make it financially viable.

I applauded that decision. I was impressed by any authority which saved the people's pennies, or *centimes*, in this case, whenever it could. These ceremonies never come cheap as nothing in this part of France ever happens without food and wine, at the very least.

I was informed that the postponed ceremony would take place in June, at the *sous-préfecture* in Ambert. That was where I had begun the process of becoming a French citizen by taking my completed forms, with all *inutile mentions* duly biffed, and being interviewed by the secretary general. I was told I was welcome to bring any family members with me to the ceremony. All would be welcome.

There was only my brother by way of family and, although we were on better terms since living far apart, with his various problems, he was not someone I would have chosen to invite to a formal ceremony. Certainly not one which meant so much to me. As it happened, the date coincided with another visit from my old and dear friend, Alex. I asked if he might be able to accompany me and was told of course, friends, family, anyone at all could attend.

I knew the ceremony would be a formal occasion, as French bureaucracy does love its formality. I had a vague notion of how things would go, as I'd done some research. But I hadn't spoken to anyone who had had a similar experience. It would be conducted by *Monsieur le sous-préfet*, the official representing the state at local level. Or in the case of Ambert at that time, by *Madame le sous-préfet.*

Alex and I scrubbed up and donned our best bibs and tuckers for the occasion. We were able to park not too far away, always handy as Alex often needs to use a wheelchair because of various smoking-related health problems like Chronic Obstructive Pulmonary Disease and Peripheral Vascular Disease. If any of you readers are still smoking, take that as a salutary warning of the dangers of the demon weed.

There were eight of us for the ceremony, and a real air of excitement about us all. I had not realised that the *maire* of each of the different communes in which we lived would also attend the ceremony, although in my case, the *maire* not being available, it was one of his deputies. In fact it was none other than 'Library Lady', the kind person who had made me so welcome and sorted me out when I first went to join the library in my new town of Olliergues.

The woman from the *sous-préfecture*, who had looked so dubious when she first handed me all the forms to biff to make my application, beamed at me proudly. Despite her doubts, I had made it, and here I was, all set for the final formalities to make me a French person.

Madame le sous-préfet was there, resplendent in her uniform, not dissimilar to that of a British naval officer. She welcomed everyone personally, then invited us to follow her to the room where the ceremony was to take place.

Alex and I exchanged a look and both our faces fell. She was heading off up quite a long, curving, flight of stairs and when I asked about a lift, I was informed that there was no disabled access to the first floor. But this was France, home of the principle of '*égalité*'. *Madame le sous-préfet* herself came back down the stairs and said if Alex couldn't manage the stairs, a way would be found to hoist him and his wheelchair aloft and get him there somehow. Spurred on by the kind offer, he managed to make his way to the top, slowly and carefully, with a few pauses to get his breath back.

The ceremony began with a short film about our new rights and responsibilities as French citizens. It was inspiring stuff. Despite not speaking much French, I could see that Alex was as engrossed in it as I was. It laid out carefully and simply for us what was expected of us, as well as what France could offer us in exchange.

Then *Madame le sous-préfet* stood up to speak. If ever the term 'motivational speaker' was thoroughly deserved, it certainly was in her case. By the time she'd finished telling us all about our duties to protect France at all costs, I was ready to attack any enemy who came near the borders of my adoptive country, single-handedly, if necessary.

If, after her speech, she had handed me a rifle and bayonet, or even a pitchfork, and told me to go and man the barricades, I would have been right there, in the front ranks. I could see from the rapt expression on Alex's face that he would have been with me, standing shoulder to shoulder, and he couldn't understand most of what she had been saying.

I was so impressed with her powers of rhetoric that I later looked her up online and found she had been a top-level athlete who, after a serious accident, had fought back to fitness and continued to compete as a Paralympian. No wonder she was good at motivating others.

After she had finished, the *maire*, or their deputy, of each commune stood up to present the certificate of citizenship to their successful candidate and to welcome them as a French national, with a kiss on both cheeks.

Of course we sang the national anthem, La Marseillaise, with its stirring and blood-thirsty lyrics, especially the call to arms, summoning citizens to form battalions, to march forth and water the furrows with impure blood.

'Aux armes, citoyens,
Formez vos bataillons,
Marchons, marchons!
Qu'un sang impur
Abreuve nos sillons!'

Whatever one's feelings about the monarchy in Britain, it has to be said that the Marseillaise is a much more stirring anthem, both in words and in music, than the dismal dirge that is 'God Save the Queen.'

It was an intensely moving experience. I think it's safe to say that all of us new 'Frogs' were full of pride in our achievement at having jumped through all the necessary hoops to officially become a part of our adoptive country.

Madame le sous-préfet is no longer in office, having moved on, but I will never forget her rousing speech. As long as I am able to get to the barricades, I would still be happy and proud to man them, in her honour, lethally-sharpened pitchfork in hand, against all invaders.

Vive la France!

Chapter Five
Fun with Rubber

Stop that sniggering at once! It's not going to be that sort of chapter. If you don't already know, our regional capital city, Clermont-Ferrand, is known as the home of the Michelin industry. And Michelin means tyres, amongst other things. Hence the rubber.

When Alex came to stay, which was often twice a year, for four weeks at a time, I always had great fun planning all the outings we would enjoy, and finding different places to visit.

The young woman at the tourist office in my home-town of Olliergues had suggested several times that I should take him to the Michelin Adventure in Clermont-Ferrand. Michelin is, of course, one of the three largest tyre manufacturers in the world. To me, it sounded about as interesting as watching paint dry. On abstract art. But Michelin also has a long history in the aviation industry, and Alex does love his planes, so we decided to give it a go.

The longer I live in the countryside, the more inept I become at driving in any town with a population of more than about five thousand. Clermont-Ferrand, our regional capital, and the biggest city in the Auvergne, boasts a population of some 140,000. Small-fry, as cities go, but certainly enough to reduce me to a gibbering idiot whenever I try to function there.

Earlier during Alex's visit, I'd been really brave and agreed that we would both meet my brother in the city centre, using the tram, to save the stress of the drive. It also appealed to my inner green, being so much less polluting. Theoretically it should be really easy, as the tramway is newish and fully equipped for wheelchair passengers, like Alex, and we could park on the edge of the city to take the tram into the centre.

I was feeling pleased with myself for having found the right place to park at the tram station, thinking I'd passed the first part of the challenge. We made our way to the ticket office to pay our fares, me clutching the car park ticket I was supposed to show at the same time as booking our tram ride.

Only when it was our turn at the window, the ticket I proudly presented turned out to be the wrong thing entirely. It was actually the ticket from another tourist attraction we'd been to, for a ride on the little tourist train round Vichy. I felt like a proper muppet!

The nice ticket man smiled with patient understanding when I explained that I was from the country, not used to these city ways. I rushed, red-face, back to the van, and scrabbled about in the usual jumble of old motorway toll tickets and toffee papers to find the missing car park ticket, which I had only just been issued with.

We managed to accomplish the rest of the journey without incident, and even to find the right stop at which to get off. It yet again illustrated how like a fish out of water I am in the city. But as the Michelin Adventure is just a stone's throw from the tram station, and I'd already managed to find my way there once, I agreed to give it a go.

It's a relatively new tourist attraction, so we were hopeful it would have good disabled facilities, and its website certainly said that it was disabled-friendly. I'd found out that the cost for old grunters like Alex and me was eight Euros each, which didn't seem too bad, so we were all set to try it out.

We arrived at the reception desk, me pushing Alex in his wheelchair, and I asked the young woman for two tickets for seniors. When she informed me that would be eight Euros, I said that it was for two of us, thinking she had misunderstood my accent. No, she reassured me, that was correct, my entry was free as I was accompanying a disabled visitor. Ten brownie points straight off, Michelin – what an excellent idea!

Disabled access to the exhibitions was no problem. A nice young man appeared, shepherded us into a special wheelchair lift, then trotted down the stairs himself to meet us and set us on our way around the attraction.

To my own surprise, I found the visit fascinating. I had been wondering how many ways there could be to present rubber in an interesting way. Now stop that at once, dear reader, I can see you sniggering again! But the history of tyres proved to be surprisingly engaging, and there were plenty of interactive games to play.

There were also some beautiful old cars and rail-cars. It was only when Alex wanted to take photos of them that he realised he had left his expensive mobile phone in the van. Not just anywhere in the van but in full view, on the dashboard. He was, of course, worried about his phone. I was worried about getting back to find a broken window, my van being parked in not a particularly salubrious part of town.

There was nothing we could do. If someone was going to steal it, they would. It may well already have been taken. We would just have to put it out of our minds and enjoy the visit, which we were doing. Every single exhibit was wheelchair accessible, which made such a pleasant change. We were able to board a rail-car and watch a video about its history. There were ramps and lifts a-plenty, so we could get wherever we wanted to be.

Michelin are, of course, also famous for their maps. There was a really interesting section on all their old motoring maps, and the days when you could get an entire itinerary for your planned journey. They were to French motoring what the RAC, the Royal Automobile Club, had been to British driving in its heyday. So much nicer than a GPS!

It's ironic that the one time we got lost finding our way around the exhibits was in trying to make our way from the map section to the souvenir shop. We had the leaflet with the floor plan in front of us, but try as we might, we kept wandering around the same dark passages without finding where we needed to be.

Finally, the mystery was solved. There was a mezzanine, which the floor plan didn't make clear. It meant finding the right lift to take us there. But soon Alex was able to buy souvenirs for his friend's children, and we both had an inexpensive and almost-drinkable coffee from a machine. Inevitably, we posed to have our photos taken with that most iconic of figures, Bibendum, the Michelin man, which was magically delivered direct to our email inboxes, in clever ways which were beyond my comprehension.

Then it was off back to find the van, both hugely relieved to discover all windows intact and the mobile phone still sitting invitingly on the dash board. I wonder if there are still cities in the UK where that would have been the case? I would like to think that there are.

One place we'd been meaning to go for some time was the industrial museum in Ambert. It's part of the same group which runs the tourist railway, which Alex and I had both ridden up to La Chaise Dieu, and which includes lots of old steam engines.

What I didn't know about Ambert is that its two main industries are weaving and making rosaries, and there were exhibits of both, which were more interesting than they sounded as if they would be. By weaving, I'm not talking anything as boring as mere cloth or yarn. No, Ambert is famous for weaving anything and everything from multi-coloured round shoe laces, to electric fencing tape, to lead ropes for horses, with all kinds of permutations in between.

The museum houses some of the weaving machinery, from different periods in history, which is still in working order. I had no idea how mesmerising it could be to watch thread flying off spinning bobbins to form a long and brightly coloured sausage which would one day be lacing up a trainer or being a pull cord for a hoody.

Not all of our visits during Alex's trips to France have been as enjoyable or successful in terms of disabled access, however. It has to be said, it's something that's still pretty much in its infancy here in the Auvergne, possibly in France in general. Newer attractions have to comply with European legislation. Old ones at best pay lip service, at worst, do nothing at all.

Our visit to discover the insides of a volcano was a good example of how it falls short in some areas. The volcano at Lemptégy has been open-cast mined, so it's possible to go round it to have a good look at its innards, and there is a train ride round it, perfect for Alex. I checked carefully on the website before we went, to make sure a wheelchair would pose no problems. The website clearly said there were two wheelchair places on the train. So off we went, full of anticipation.

The entrance was rather rough for wheelchairs, and very dusty, with all the dust at just the wrong height for anyone unfortunate enough to be sitting down. Undaunted, we bought our tickets for the visit, which began with a 3-D film all about the volcano's history, followed by the guided train tour.

The film was brilliant! We both sat spellbound, like two little kids, in the theatre seats, leaving Alex's chair to one side. That way we experienced all the thrill of the show, from being shaken by 'eruptions' to having our faces wafted with hot air or sprayed with water and icy blasts. We felt as if we really were right there when our local volcanoes last erupted, some of them less than ten thousand years ago. Most are extinct, although several are classified as dormant so could, in theory, erupt again at any time.

From there, we made our way down to the platform to board the train. We were rather surprised, and a little bit disconcerted, when the train driver, who was also the tour guide, insisted that we left the chair on the platform. Alex was understandably worried about its security and it also meant he would be unable to get out and move about, if there was anywhere to do so. But the driver was adamant.

We couldn't understand why, as the website clearly said there were wheelchair places on the train. In any event, we were sitting alone in a small compartment meant to accommodate more than just Alex and me, so we could easily have folded the chair up and put it in with us. But no, we were not allowed to.

The train is on wheels, not tracks, not restricted to following rails, so off we trundled on our way. The driver/guide kept up an extremely detailed running commentary all the way round the tour, which took over an hour. It was interesting, but the commentary was literally non-stop, leaving me no time at all to translate adequately for Alex, without losing the thread of what the guide was saying. There were also endless figures, dates, quantities, heights, weights and the like and, being slightly dyscalculic, I struggle with those in English, never mind when doing simultaneous translation into French.

There were a couple of stops along the way where Alex was at least able to get down and walk a few metres to take some photos, though with nothing like the independence and mobility the chair would have given him.

We came to a place which looked very interesting, with all the old mine machinery still in place. As the train stopped, there was a lot of chatter amongst the passengers so I could barely hear what the guide was saying about the length of the stop. Alex and I got off, along with most of the passengers, then the train went on its way, with just a handful of people still on it.

Alex started to panic, thinking he'd been abandoned. I reassured him that the train was sure to come back for us – I thought I'd heard the driver say so. But no. She had apparently been saying she wasn't coming back so only the truly able-bodied should disembark.

I had to run after her to get her to return for Alex, which she did with very bad grace, saying it was our own fault for getting off. Useless me pointing out to her that she knew she had a disabled wheelchair user on board as she had confiscated his wheelchair, and she also knew he was English, so should have checked that he had understood and had not got off.

Worse was to come. The train, not restricted to following tracks, didn't return to the platform from which we had departed, but set us down somewhere else, with a fence and a one-way locked gate between us and the wheelchair. There was no way Alex could have gone in pursuit of his chair himself.

I could go and get it, but once having gone through the gate, I would need someone to press the locking mechanism from the inside to let me back in, and it was too far for Alex to walk to do so. Thanks to the unfailing kindness of French people around us, who, seeing our predicament, leapt to our assistance, we managed. Just as well, as our driver/guide had simply driven off with the train to begin the next tour, without even checking to make sure we were sorted.

No point in me complaining at the ticket desk, either. I got short shrift there, just being told that disabled visitors had to be accompanied. So much for *égalité* there, then.

Chapter Six
Say Cheese!

It's no exaggeration to say that cheese is a part of the way of life in France, especially in the Auvergne. France is said to have a different variety of cheese for every day of the year. I would suggest that's an under-estimate.

Here in the Auvergne, there are five principle AOC cheeses, AOC being *Appellation d'origine contrôlée*, literally 'controlled designation of origin'. AOC is why the French refuse to allow wines to be called champagne unless they come from the Champagne region, for example. It sets down clear and rigorous standards for products. In the case of the cheese, it can include such things as the altitude at which the cattle must graze and the wild plants to which they must have access.

Our Famous Five in the cheese world are Cantal, which is a little bit like Cheddar and comes in three stages of maturity, Salers, a similar cheese but with more specific requirements in production, Saint Nectaire, a creamy cheese a little like a Brie, and the two blue cheeses, Fourme d'Ambert and Bleu d'Auvergne.

In addition, we have so many local varieties and variations on a theme that it would fill this chapter to list them. Even our small cheese shop in the little town of Olliergues has more varieties than you might find on the average supermarket cheese counter in the UK. They include cows' milk, goats' milk, sheep's milk, and mixes thereof, whites and blues, strong and mild, smoked and unsmoked, hard or creamy.

Cheese here is eaten as a separate course, often at both lunch and dinner/supper/tea or whatever you like to call it in your household. Trying to explain to English learners the different names the English have for meals at different times of day is a headache in itself.

It is eaten after the main course and before the dessert, as a palate cleanser, and always on its own. No bread, no crackers, not even a grape or two, and never, ever with pineapple chunks. What a strange fashion that was! Lumps of cheese and cubes of pineapple on cocktail sticks, all stuck into a grapefruit like a hedgehog. I suspect it would be illegal here. About as affronting as pineapple on a pizza is to the Italians.

But slowly, the Auvergnats are venturing boldly into the idea of combining cheese with something a little fruity. You can even buy various chutneys now, designed to be served with cheese, although most of the locals I see give those a very wide berth when they pass the shelves. I like to eat my cheese with mango chutney, but I do it in the privacy of my own home, for fear my French citizenship will be revoked, should my guilty secret ever get out.

As I was patiently queuing in the cheese shop one morning – they have patient queuing off to a fine art here, you hardly ever hear any huffing or tutting – the lady behind the counter was helping a man to make his selection. One cheese had a vein of a deep pink colour waving its way artistically through it, which gave it a lovely marbled effect. It was, explained the lady, a vein of pressed grapes running through the cheese, to add a little variety of flavour.

The man gave her what I can only describe as an old-fashioned look and said, patiently enough, 'Madame, if I wish to eat grapes, I will eat grapes. I wish to eat cheese,' which summed up perfectly the tradionalists' suspicion of anything 'fancy' going on with their cheese.

I was actually queuing for a daring new speciality they

have started doing in the local shop – *chevre enrobé*, coated goats' cheese. A deliciously tasty new delicacy, consisting of a small round of mild goats' cheese, sitting in one of those little paper cases you use for cupcakes, with the sides of the cheese coated in a dried fruit crust of your choice. My particular favourite is *exotique*, which is dried mango and papaya, closely followed by cranberry and kumquat..

If you'd told me, when I first moved to France more than eight years ago, that I would one day be buying something as exotic as that in the local shop, I would have laughed at you. They don't seem to sell a lot of them, and I suspect I may buy most of them. But there they sit, comfortably rubbing shoulders with the more traditional '*briques*' of goat and ewes' milk cheese, sporting their layer of grape or pineapple, redcurrant or exotic fruits.

Cheese is one of the big attractions which draws my friend Alex back to the Auvergne again and again. He loves coming to see the dogs, to visit the war museums and battle sites. I hope he also quite likes coming to see me. But no visit of his is complete without eating a lot of cheese, and buying a few big lumps to take back home with him. Not quite as straightforward as you might imagine.

Poor Alex has had more than his fair share of adventures in getting out to visit me by public transport. Despite always organising disabled assistance for him, as he simply cannot walk far and needs to use his wheelchair, the help is not always there when needed. When it is there, it is not always well thought out.

Pointless to park a wheelchair user, alone and without access to their wheelchair, in the middle of a busy airport terminal during a long lay-over, miles from the nearest loo or food outlet. He's had that experience on one occasion and we've had to complain long and hard about it. We got an apology, an assurance it would not happen again and a voucher towards his next flight.

SAY CHEESE!

Recently, obsessive airport security has been providing a few unexpected problems. I can understand the need for security on planes, after recent terrorist attacks and attempts, I really can. But sometimes the rules do seem a bit strange.

No cheese in your hand luggage. Right, ok. I know some French cheeses are particularly pungent – one of Napolean's favourits, Époisses, is banned on public transport, for example – but would our Auvergne cheese be strong enough to render the cabin crew unconcious? It would seem so, as on one homeward bound trip, Alex was made to lock his Cantal and Salers firmly into his baggage destined to go in the hold.

The only trouble is, the one thing most dogs cannot resist is cheese. Even trained guard dogs, who cannot be bribed with meat, with sometimes sell their soul for a lump of cheese, the stinkier the better. This clearly applies to sniffer dogs at airports.

When Alex went to recover his case on reaching Birmingham Airport, he found the lid had been ripped off and all trace of his delicious cheese had disappeared. Nothing else was touched. All his other belongings and presents were intact, so the suspicion had to fall on those sniffer dogs, who clearly enjoyed an unexpected feast of Auvergnat cheese.

Another complaint to Air France, another flight voucher for Alex's collection. At this rate, they were going to be paying him to fly with them!

On another occasion the new rule was no wild boar paté in the cabin, even if hermetically sealed into a jar and clearly unopened. Presumably, said jar could be used to club the cabin crew over the head into unconsciousness, prior to storming the flight deck.

I'm not in any way trivialising recent tragic events on aircraft. But Alex and I know from experience just how difficult those paté jars are to open. When we were heading off on one of our frequent picnics, Alex spotted them in the supermarket as we shopped for our lunch and decided to give one a try.

We were sitting happily on top of a strategic high point, south of Clermont-Ferrand, allegedly the site of the big battle between the Arveni chief Vercingétorix and the Roman soldiers of Julius Caesar's Gallic Wars. We spread out our feast on a picnic table, crusty bread and a jar of paté for Alex, boring old cardboard maize crackers for me, because of Silly Coeliac disease.

It was one of those jars with a metal fastening that you somehow have to flip open and wiggle about to get it to cede and let you take the lid off. Alex tried. I tried. I got my trusty big knife, which goes everywhere with me, and tried with that.

Eventually, between us, through brute force and ignorance, we got the lid off and Alex enjoyed his lunch. But it would be a very determined terrorist indeed who would succeed in tampering with one of those jars. There must surely be easier ways of taking down an aircraft.

On this occasion, security at the airport didn't even offer him the option of putting the offending item into his hold luggage instead. They simply confiscated it. Somebody in security had a nice supper that day, and Auvergnat wild boar paté is not exactly something Alex can easily find on the shelf of his local supermarket in Birmingham.

Chapter Seven
Take Three Birds

Do you instinctively groan when a friend utters the words, 'I've had a great idea'? I suppose it depends on the friend. But when my friend Jilli said that, or rather, typed that, in a Facebook message, I certainly did groan.

Jilli, is not the Jill you have met in the other *Sell the Pig* books, my best friend for many a year. Jilli lives in Italy and up to this point, we had never met in the flesh.

For some reason, it seemed to cause great confusion that I had two friends called Jill. Or perhaps people were surprised that I have friends at all! Just to make it easier to follow, old friend from Wales is always called Jill, newer friend from Italy is Jilli or Doris, as she is affectionately known, as she can be a reet dozy Doris, as they say 'oop north', .

I first got to know Italy Jilli through a now defunct online site for writers, Authonomy.com, where wannabe authors could post their works in progress for the critique of others. Jilli and I read each other's books, then started chatting and finally met up on Facebook. We began to chat there regularly and quickly started to call one another 'bird', a slang word for woman, which is often used to hide a touch of affection.

Jilli become Doris Bird, I was Tottie Bird and another friend, who soon became part of the gang, was Posh Bird. We'd spend long hours talking, or rather, typing, and laughing via Facebook messenger. It often got hysterically funny, especially when the other two had been drinking and I was the sober one. Sadly, I can no longer drink more than a teaspoonful at a time or my legs start being silly. I just seem to have lost all tolerance for it, probably because of debauchery in my early journalist days.

I'm just going to say at the outset that it's not my intention to repeat here everything that's already been written in the book which emerged from this brilliant idea. If you want to know more, I suggest you buy Take Three Birds by Jilli Lime-Holt, the collective name for the Three Birds. This is just the bare bones of it all.

Jilli's bright idea was that the three of us should get together and write a book, but that we should all attempt to meet up somewhere in the flesh in order to write about our meeting. I knew Jilli could write as I had read her book, 'Diary of a single parent abroad'. It was a good book, although in need of some serious editing, which I offered to do for her.

If you like memoirs, or any inspiring real-life tale, it's certainly that. Shortly after Jilli moved to live in Italy, with three small children in tow, her husband went back to the UK to live with another woman. Jilli was alone and pretty much destitute, in a run-down house in the middle of nowhere, in a foreign land.

Many women would simply have taken the easy option of fleeing back to Blighty, or as she likes to call it, Shitey Blighty. Not our Doris! The length she went to to bring up three great kids with next to no means was truly inspirational.

Posh Bird was articulate, intelligent, could string words together and had previously had some poetry published, so it sounded like a possibility. As for the where we should meet up, that was more or less pre-determined. I don't travel much at all these days, and could certainly not contemplate leaving my dogs.

My two rescued border collies, Ci and Fleur, had each come with their own personal baggage. This meant that either putting them in kennels or getting a dog-sitter for them was out of the question, to me. Ci didn't like strangers, especially strange men, at all. Fleur has the looks of an angel but the heart of a devil. She is, as the Irish say, a little fecker, meaning she runs off at the least opportunity.

She's not good with other dogs and is also rabidly racist. She hates vehemently, though not exclusively, Golden Retrievers, white Swiss Shepherds, Australian Shepherds and most German breeds. It makes walking her interesting, to say the least.

That effectively narrowed the choice down to one. The others would have to come and stay with me in France. To make it more interesting, I suggested that Posh Bird should fly first to Italy, to Jilli's house, then she and Doris Bird could do a 'Thelma and Louise' type road trip, hopefully without the canyon scene, to come and stay with me.

All systems were go, it seemed.

Then personal circumstances meant Posh Bird had to pull out. Jilli was still determined that the project should go ahead and, being a masochist as well as slightly deranged, had set us a target of writing the book and getting it out in time for Christmas. That gave us about four months in total.

We recruited a new Third Bird, also from the Authonomy site. Farmer Bird was not a writer, but her ghost-written tale was a good one and we knew she could certainly tell a story. The mere detail that she had never before flown and didn't even possess a passport wasn't going to stop a Determined Doris in her tracks. So the crazy idea was back on.

My main preoccupation was how I was going to accommodate two complete strangers in my tiny grottage without Ci feeling the need to eat either of them. Both were doggy people so should they should, in theory, get on with him. But Ci loved to sleep on the very narrow landing just outside the guest room door. There was the strong possibility that, should either of them need the bathroom in the night, they might forget he was there, tread on him and get bitten.

I was also not sure that asking the two of them to share a bedroom after a long drive in a small car all the way from Italy was going to be ideal. They, too, had never met before, and would have spent just a couple of nights in each other's company before setting off. By the time they arrived, after an estimated eight-hour drive, they might be as likely to bite one another as Ci was to bite them, if the journey had been fraught.

To be fair to Ci, he had recently shown signs of improvement with strangers. Luckily, as it turned out. I had spent a lot of time mucking out the old cow shed underneath the hay loft in my barn. It made a cool, roomy and, I thought, secure place to put the dogs on a hot or a rainy day, especially if there were people about.

My kind friends Geoff and Christine, had given me an elderly gas cooker for my kitchen when I first moved to my grottage, for days when it was too hot to light Kevin the Kitchen Range. It was also valuable back-up for when Kevin was being his typical stroppy teenage self and refusing to go. But the gas cooker was not all that accurate and, being quite old, it had the gas cylinder inside it, which is no longer permitted. The gas bottle is now meant to be stored outside the house, for safety reasons, with the pipe running through the exterior wall.

I decided to invest in something more modern and reliable, especially for baking. I love making cakes but was getting too many disappointing results, between Kevin and the gas cooker. I picked out an efficient-looking Bosch at my local shop and arranged to have that delivered and fitted, with the gas cannister outside the house, as required. This would necessitate drilling through the extremely thick outer wall. The cooker had an electric oven and one electric hotplate, plus three gas rings, so should, in theory, give me different options.

As a quick aside, I sometimes get into hot debates with British expats in France on social media sites who claim all

French workmen are unreliable. It's not my experience here. The two men who delivered Bruno the Bosch, and installed him, were excellent. They arrived on time, they coped with the fact that their brief was incorrect and they didn't have the right equipment with them. They also coped with Ci.

I'd put Ci and Fleur in the cowshed, which I thought was secure. That way they wouldn't be barking at the men all the time as they were coming and going, as they would do if I put them in the small pen in the garden, where they would be looking at them all the time. So hopefully, Ci would be safely out of sight, out of mind and not too stressed by intruders on his territory.

I was, as usual, at my desk in the kitchen, writing, with the back door open to the garden. The two men were coming and going between the kitchen and their van in search of different tools. Out of the corner of my eye, I just happened to see a small, black ballistic missile, hurtling up the garden with murderous intent. Ci had escaped from the cowshed!

In a panic, I shot out of the door just as Ci reached one of the men who, fortunately, did the sensible thing and stood stock still, hands by his sides and not making any eye contact with the ferociously barking ball of black fur hurtling towards him. I called out to him not to move and he assured me in a quiet voice he had no intention of doing so.

Ci was so surprised he also just stood still, woofing a bit at the immobile man who luckily stayed true to his word and was not moving a muscle. Ci was showing no signs of attack, as long as the man didn't move, so I was able to round him up and put him back in the cowshed. I hastily did running repairs on my infamous BIY – Bodge-it-Yourself – to make it more secure, and luckily it held long enough for the cooker to be installed.

To avoid any possible repeat performance inside the confines of the house, I decided the best thing would be to give the two visiting Birds a bedroom each and for me and the dogs to move into a tent in the garden. Not a hardship for any of us, since we all loved camping and often did it.

I chose the biggest and poshest of my four tents, one with two bedrooms and a dining area, got it set up and we started sleeping in it the week before the Birds were due to arrive. We were having great fun, it was so nice to be camping again.

Then one night, just as we were going to sleep, Ci started coughing a bit, as if he had something stuck in his throat. I couldn't see anything, but he kept doing it. We moved back into the house, so there was better light for me to keep an eye on him. I decided we'd spend the night in the sitting room as he sounded as if he wanted to be sick and that way, we were handy for the door, so he could go out.

By about five in the morning, he was starting to have difficulty breathing, so I phoned my vet, who was always so good at handling him. Only he wasn't there. I left a message on his answer-phone. Ci was getting worse, so I clearly couldn't wait for his return call. I looked in the yellow pages, not knowing who else to call as we had always used the same vet.

I phoned one in Ambert, told them that Ci now appeared to be seriously ill and that I hoped to be there in just over half an hour. What a nightmare journey it turned out to be! Fleur always barks like a mad thing when in the van, which did nothing for my already jangled nerves. On an early autumnal morning, the river valley route down to Ambert was swirling with thick mist, which slowed me to a crawl in places. Plus the town itself had the dreaded *déviations*, diversions, all over everywhere and I got horribly lost.

In desperation I phoned the vet for directions but she, by now very grumpy, had gone back home as I was so late. Luckily, I managed to convince her how serious it was and she came back to the surgery to meet me and helped me to carry Ci, now in a bad way, inside.

She diagnosed pulmonary oedema, fluid in the lungs, and said his airways were seriously compromised. She was kindness itself while she fought hard to stabilise my beloved dog, tubing him to get vital oxygen into his lungs, and still finding time to make me some calming green tea.

She suspected a severe asthma attack, possibly heart failure, but got him to the point where she said it would be better for me to take him home, with more heart medication, then bring him back the next morning for further tests and more treatment. She was on her own, on Sunday duty, and didn't want to have to leave him unattended if she got a call-out.

Every breath was causing him difficulty, so Fleur and I stayed with him all the time to reassure him once we got home. That evening, I once again bedded down on the settee, with Ci on the floor by my side, his breathing noisy and laboured. He still had a cannula in his leg, ready for more medication the next morning.

Around midnight, as I was trying to get some rest, I felt Ci, as he so often did, jump up next to me and snuggle down between me and the back of the settee, with a lovely, warm, comforting feeling. He gave a yelp as he did so, as if the cannula had hurt him when he jumped.

I lay a moment, waiting for him to draw the next breath. It never came. I reached out a hand to feel him. There was no heartbeat, no rise and fall of his chest. At last, the terribly laboured breathing had stopped. My little buddy had gone. Only eight years old, and with no prior warning.

Opening my home to welcome in two complete strangers so soon afterwards, still feeling so raw and emotional, was one of the hardest things I have ever done. We wrote the book, we made our impossible self-set deadline, and it was a modest success.

My French antique mantel clock, which had kept perfect time and soothed me with its delightful chimes ever since I moved to France, was behind the settee when Ci died there. It has steadfastly refused to go at all, ever since.

Chapter Eight
Hello in There

Although I cried myself to sleep in the tent every night while my visitors were here, I didn't really feel I could grieve properly until they were bundled into their little Fiat and heading for the motorway which would take them back to Italy. Unless, of course they got as spectacularly lost as they did on the outward bound journey (all is revealed in Take Three Birds).

Once they'd left, Fleur and I were on our own, for the first time ever. I was worried about how Fleur would adjust to suddenly being an only dog. She was clearly missing Ci, her 'big brother', as much as I was, but fortunately, she showed no signs of separation anxiety when I went out and had to leave her alone in the house.

I would just put the television on for company, give her a treat and leave her to settle down until I got back. Nothing was ever chewed up, no puddles awaiting my return, thankfully. In a way, she seemed to be quite enjoying her time as an only dog. It was such a relief as, with her incessant barking in the car, she's not always an easy dog to take on a long journey, so it's easier to leave her at home when I'm not going to be too long.

I never thought there could be a positive side to losing Ci, but in a sense, being without him helped me get to know my neighbours a little better. Ci's defensive aggression towards strangers meant that it was always difficult in the extreme to stop and talk to people. He would bark, snarl and swear horribly at anyone who dared approach me, his beloved mistress. His self-appointed task had always been, from the moment I got him, to protect me from anyone and anything, even if they posed no real threat.

Fleur, on the other hand, loves all people regardless and is hugely sociable. Thirty seconds in her company and you find yourself wearing her like a scarf. Suddenly, walking round the lanes, just the two of us, we found ourselves able to stop and chat to people, who were always delighted by how pretty Fleur was, and how very friendly, always so licky and waggy. Her caramel-coloured eyes always look as if they have been outlined with a kohl pencil, just like a Bollywood star.

The place where I live is too small to be classed even as a hamlet. It is a *Lieu Dit*, literally, a 'place known as', and comprises less than a couple of dozen houses. The average age of the population is high, with several of the residents well into their eighties. One or two come up only for the summer, preferring to go back to town for the winter, which can be harsh here.

Walking with blonde, beautiful Fleur by my side, I found that some of the older residents would come out of their front doors to engage us in conversation. I find it a charming part of French life that I am always greeted with, 'Bonjour, madame,' even by people older than I. I think that formality is so nice, and it's always delivered with a warm smile, at least around here.

Now our walks were taking much longer because we would have to stop and chat on our way round, but how nice that was. And I now had the time to spare, as I'd finally decided, in July 2014, that I'd had enough of working for a living and had retired. No more silly deadlines to meet. Now the only writing I did was what I wanted to do, my books, my blog and articles for various websites.

Fleur was rapidly becoming a bit of a local celebrity. She was quite happy to sit and be stroked by any number of the elderly ladies we met. One of them was particularly delighted, as she had a small grand-daughter who was also called Fleur.

I started making a point of passing at a time when the older ladies might be sitting on their front porch, just so we could pass the time of day. It was great practice for my French, a chance to learn a bit more about my adoptive area and also, it put me in mind of a beautiful song by John Prine, Hello In There. It talks of the loneliness of older people, often living alone, and just waiting for someone to stop by to say hello. Fleur and I were happy to fill that role.

It was a good job that Fleur showed she could safely be left alone, because of a change in travel arrangements for Alex's visits. He'd always flown into Clermont-Ferrand's Aulnat airport, an easy drive of less than an hour for me to go and pick up him. But because of all the problems he had experienced with disabled assistance with the change of aircraft at Paris, he had decided instead to try flying direct from Birmingham to Lyon instead.

Lyon is the twin city of Birmingham, since they are both second cities of their respective countries, so there are regular, inexpensive flights between them. It meant a much longer drive for me, a good two and a half hours each way, but it was certainly worth a try.

The first time I made the journey, I decided to take Fleur with me, despite the barking, as it would be a long time to leave her home alone. I hadn't been to Lyon airport for about ten years, since Jill and I flew in there on our fact-finding mission round the Auvergne. Being a compulsive planner, I did a lot of searching on the Internet to make sure I knew exactly how to get to the airport and where best to park, so I wouldn't be all of a fluster on arrival. I knew it had expanded considerably since the last time I had been there.

Fleur and I left in plenty of time, typically for me, to allow for several stops for walkies for Fleur, and to be sure of finding the right parking place. I thought I had worked out most eventualities. What I hadn't correctly factored in, however, was how busy it was at Lyon since my last visit there, being used to our small, single runway airport in Clermont-Ferrand.

We arrived at the right car park with no trouble, but I found myself having to drive round and round in endless descending spirals, seemingly down into the bowels of the earth, before I could find a parking space. And that in turn meant that poor Fleur had to ride in a scary lift to get us back up to the level of the terminal. Bless her, despite clearly being more than a little afraid, she behaved perfectly.

A little later than we planned, and more than a little rattled by things not having gone quite according to plan, we arrived at the terminal just as my mobile phone starting to ring in my pocket. When I answered, Alex's voice told me to turn around and there he was, beaming widely and being pushed towards me in his wheelchair. It was great to see him again.

A friend had given me a really good route to get to the airport via St Etienne, but Alex was dying to show off the GPS app on his posh phone, so he insisted on setting that to navigate us back home. No use me saying that the dozy Doris who was directing us had told us to take the wrong exit from the motorway at one point. The app was accurate, I was told.

By this time we were wandering into some not at all pleasant-looking areas round the back of Lyon and had lost all signs to our destination. Matters were made worse when the route we had been told to take took us through a series of tunnels, at which point the GPS simply abandoned us and refused to talk to us again through lack of a signal.

I made an executive decision and backtracked to where it had first taken us the wrong way, then steadfastly ignored the GPS's increasingly insistent orders to do an about turn, as we had left the tunnels behind and it was happy to talk to us again. I simply followed the signs to places I recognised. It just confirmed my belief that GPSs and I were never meant to be together.

The fact that we'd had the stress of the car park and nearly getting lost did nothing for poor Fleur's barking, just making her do it all the more. I decided that if Lyon airport was going to be the best bet for Alex, I would just have to leave Fleur at home while I did the journey as quickly as possible, which is what I did for the return trip there. She was fine, quite happily installed watching UK television. BBC, of course. I refuse to let her watch ITV, as I consider things like the Jeremy Kyle show not suitable for her delicate sensibilities.

As well as getting to know my neighbours a little better, my walks with Fleur also helped me to see more of the local wildlife, of which there was always plenty. In particular, there is a real feral cat problem around here, with so many of them.

Don't let anyone tell you the French are not a nation of animals lovers to rival the British. My neighbour is a particular soft touch for any animal in need. She already feeds a collection of feral cats, and has sorted out getting them neutered, in an attempt to restrict their numbers.

One day, as Fleur and I were walking along the quiet lane on our way back to the house, a young tortoiseshell cat flew out of the undergrowth, all snarls, spits and swearing, and made a very determined show of seeing off Fleur and me. Tortoiseshell cats are almost always female. Males are extremely rare and usually sterile. I strongly suspected this one had kittens nearby that she was protecting.

A couple of days later, Fleur and I were walking along the same route. This time, it was not a spitting mother cat who flew out but a tiny little kitten, another tortie, all on her own, who trotted hopefully after Fleur, clearly looking for her mother.

A quick scout around confirmed my fears. Mother cat had met her end on the road so baby kitten was now on her own. Time to summon the aid of my kindly neighbour. First we put some food out for *Petit Bout de Chou*, Little Poppet, as I named the kitten, to get her used to us. She seemed heartily relieved to have found some grown-ups to take care of her, being too young to survive on her own.

Then we attempted to catch her. Not as easy as it may sound. I didn't know small kittens could fly, but this one did, very effectively, right over the top of my neighbour Chantal's head, the first time we tried to corner her. But Chantal is made of stern stuff when it comes to helping animals. This is the lady who, when a neighbour's cat she was feeding managed to get itself stuck up on the roof of their three-storey house, simply borrowed a local builder's long ladder, shinned up and brought the grateful cat down.

She was the one who finally cornered and captured *Petit Bout*. I then took the kitten to the animal refuge and was later told she had had no trouble in finding a new home very quickly. She was rather sweet.

I had to call on Chantal's help another time when Fleur and I unexpectedly found ourselves with a lodger. Fleur was barking at the garden gate one day and when I went to look, there was a friendly-looking dog outside the garden. She was not one either Chantal or I recognised and she wasn't wearing an ID tag.

Chantal's car is smart, quite new, and always immaculate. It gets a regular going over inside with the vacuum cleaner every weekend. I've had Roo the Kangoo, my van nearly four years now and it's never met a vacuum cleaner. But it was Chantal to the rescue once more, with a stray dog to be seen to. She kindly drove me and the dog to the vet to check for a microchip, but the stray was neither chipped nor tattooed. Nor had she been reported missing when we checked with the police and the *mairie* (town hall).

I offered to hang on to her until the owner reappeared, but Alex was visiting and we had a trip away planned. Chantal to the rescue yet again. I would leave Stray Dog in the secure run in the garden, and my kind neighbour would feed her the couple of nights we were away.

Luckily, her owner turned up and she was thrilled to see him again so went on her way. But watching the way that Fleur had interacted with her, playing wonderful, mad chase games like she use to play with Ci, made me realise that I wasn't being entirely fair to her.

I was being selfish, still feeling too raw to bring another dog into the house so soon after losing Ci. Fleur clearly needed a replacement playmate. It was time to start looking about to see if there was a dog somewhere, in need of a home, which might fill the void in both our lives.

Chapter Nine
Don't Mention the War

France's history in the Second World War is complicated and chequered, and no more so than in the Auvergne. On the one hand, there was the infamous Vichy government, which cooperated with the Nazis. On the other, there were the brave members of the Resistance, the Maquis, many of them just boys, who gave their lives trying to prevent more Germans from reaching the Normandy beaches.

My friend Alex is deeply interested in war history, so his visits often revolve around trips to museums and memorials. I enjoy going with him as I'm anxious to learn as much as I can about my adoptive country and its history.

The kind and helpful people in the local tourist office are always suggesting more places where I could take him. One of those they mentioned was a private collection, near to the attractive town of Brioude in the Haute Loire *département* of the Auvergne. We decided to have a run out there one day, on one of Alex's visits.

I had been told that because it was a private collection, although it is open to the public, it was worth phoning in advance to check that it was open the day we planned to visit. As it would take us the best part of a couple of hours each way, I did phone ahead and was told it would be open.

I don't often venture out of my own *département* of the Auvergne, and haven't often visited the Haute Loire. The first thing we noticed when we crossed over the county line was a compulsion to drive even more in the centre of the road than they do here. Going over a narrow bridge, with a stone parapet either side, situated on a sharp bend, was interesting indeed when we experienced a close encounter of very nearly the worst kind with an oncoming local driver.

I avoided him, and I'm still not sure how. He simply continued happily on his way, seemingly without a care in the world and certainly blissfully oblivious to the fact that he had so nearly caused an accident.

We found the museum easily enough, next to a bar. It was a warm day and turning thundery, so as my dog, Fleur, is pitifully afraid of thunder, I was keen to park somewhere I could keep a close eye on her. The museum was up a steep flight of stairs in what looked like an old hay loft, and I had to ask at the bar for them to unlock it for us.

The man who owns and runs the museum was down his garden, tending the vegetables, but appeared in response to a summons and let us in. He turned out to be the son-in-law of the man who had been the Maquis commander for the whole area, someone Alex had heard of through his research into the war history of the region.

As with any occupied country, there had been those who collaborated with the occupying German forces, and those who had chosen to side with, and fight for, the Resistance. Of course once France was liberated, there were many who claimed to have fought as part of the Maquis who had never done so, and who may well have been '*collabos*' instead.

There is still a lot of bad feeling, still many families and neighbours split by the old history of who fought for which side, who did what and, especially, who betrayed whom.

The museum owner was, of course, a fount of knowledge. He was also delighted to discover that not only was Alex interested in war history but that his father had both driven a flail tank on the Normandy beaches and had been one of the liberating forces at Bergen-Belsen concentration camp.

The two of them really wanted to chat to one another, but neither spoke the other's language well enough to make much progress by themselves. I interpreted between them as best I could, since the man spoke with the rapidity of machine-gun fire, with hardly a pause for breath and no gaps to allow me to catch him up.

Inevitably, once the man learned that I lived in France and was not just a visitor, he wanted to know where I lived. When I told him, I thought Alex and I would never get away, and it became positively embarrassing.

'Madame X was a collaborator, you know, and Monsieur Y helped the Germans, giving up the names of neighbours who were then taken away. Then there was Madame P and Monsieur Q, I could tell you things about both of them ...' and so on, until, although most of the names meant little to me, I was starting to feel uncomfortable.

Nevertheless the visit itself was interesting and the large loft was crammed full of all sorts of exhibits, so we voted it a worthwhile trip out.

No visit to war memorials in France could be considered properly complete without going to Oradour-sur-Glane in the Haute-Vienne *département* of the Limousin. It was the scene of a Nazi atrocity in June 1944, when a Waffen-SS company massacred 642 men, women and children, and burned an entire village.

A new village was constructed nearby after the war but, on the orders of the then French president Charles de Gaulle, the original site has been maintained as a permanent memorial and museum. There is now a large and impressive new visitor centre at the entrance to the 'martyr village'.

I found out from English friends, Avril and Jeremy, who live in Olliergues, that our little local town so nearly suffered the same fate as Oradour during the war. It seems that a train loaded with German troops was heading north and stopped for some reason in Olliergues.

Local children started to throw stones at the soldiers on board who then got off the train and began to give chase. The children fled into the hills. Olliergues is built down in the valley of the River Dore and has steep, sometimes terraced, hills surrounding it, where it sits on an ox-bow on the river.

The steep hills are a warren of caves and hiding places which the children knew well, fortunately, as they fled there to conceal themselves. The outcome could still have been grim indeed except that officers called back the troops, anxious to press on with their journey north, probably going as reinforcements to Normandy. So our small town was spared. Not so Oradour-sur-Glane.

We knew our visit to Oradour would be harrowing, so we made plans to temper it by combining the trip with a chance to visit dear friends, Tom and Chrissie, who were currently living in the Limousin. To make a real outing of it, we would find hotels in and around the Limousin capital, Limoges, to break our journey, as it would be a long old haul.

I'd made a brief visit to the Limousin once before but this would be Alex's first visit there. We headed first for a budget hotel near to Limoges for our first night. From there we would be no more than a stone's throw from Oradour for the next day.

Alex and I are old friends of many years' standing, but only friends, definitely nothing more. However for reasons of economy we have, on occasion shared a hotel room with separate beds, which is what we found that night. It was definitely in the 'cheap and cheerful' bracket, but fine for our needs.

There's never any point in me booking a hotel breakfast. With the constraints of my Silly Coeliac diet, there is seldom anything I can safely eat, so we generally take a kettle for drinks, never provided in the budget hotels, and take in our own food. It means a lot of kit to haul with us everywhere but it's better than the side effects for me of accidentally eating anything containing even traces of gluten.

As we had imagined, visiting Oradour was a sobering experience. Neither of us was quite prepared for the scale of the atrocity. To see what had clearly been a lively and prosperous village, with its bars, cafés, school and shops, left a blackened ruin, roofs fallen in, walls partially collapsed, was intensely moving. Many of the killings of the women and children had happened in the church, still partially standing as a sober reminder of what mankind was capable of.

There were a lot of visitors there and almost all were respecting the signs requesting quiet and no photographs. There are always a few, of course, who cannot resist any opportunity for a selfie, no matter how solemn an occasion or how inappropriate a location.

From there, we travelled further north to our next budget hotel, not far from where we were going to be meeting up with Tom and Chrissie, and there we ran into a problem. I'd booked online, but there had been nowhere to specify particular needs. Our choice was limited to a room with two beds but on the top floor and there was no lift, just a series of fire-escape style rickety stairs. Or a room on the ground floor with only one bed. A double.

I went back to the van to check with Alex on his preference. The horror on his face at the prospect of sharing a bed was hardly flattering. But one thing we'd already discovered about the Limousin was that the climate was not at all kind to his Chronic Obstructive Pulmonary Disease. It was damp and heavy. I have slight asthma, which barely ever troubles me in the clean air of the Auvergne. But even I felt I was attempting to breathe in and out through treacle with the atmosphere there. There was no way Alex could contemplate that many flights of stairs. We would just have to share like grown-ups.

I was quick to assure him I had absolutely no designs on his body, having managed very nicely without it for more than thirty years, and that all that I had in mind was to take an antihistamine to knock myself out for a peaceful sleep.

As it happened, neither of us had anything to worry about. Fleur, somehow managing to understand that things were not as they normally were, and perhaps sensing Alex's unrest, immediately jumped right into the middle of the bed and stretched out full length like a bolster.

There would be no nocturnal hanky-panky on her watch, thank you very much!

Chapter Ten
A Kiss from a Rose

Ear-worms are a major affliction for me. You know, those tunes that worm their way into your brain, usually as a result of a word you've heard or a few bars of music, and then they are stuck there for hours.

It's almost like a form of Tourette's syndrome, as I seem to have no conscious control of what pops out of my mouth, sometimes with embarrassing consequences. I've usually no idea what I have started to sing or to hum until, in a light-bulb moment, I suddenly realise that it could be unfortunate.

Luckily, most of the ear-worms which affect me are in English, so I get away with it here, where not many people speak English.

My poor dogs usually finish up with a tune dedicated to them as a result of some ear-worm or another which wriggled into what I laughingly call my brain and stayed there. Poor Ci, whose name, the Welsh word for dog, is pronounced like the French word *qui*, meaning who, was saddled with the theme music to a French children's cartoon series of the 1980s. Les Snorky had the words:

'Qui Qui Qui sont les Snorkies?' - Who Who Who are the Snorkies – as the first line of its theme song and I can't count the number of times I've sung it to my poor boy.

Despite Fleur's best effort at cheering me up with cuddles and playing with toys, I was still missing Ci dreadfully after his sudden demise. So after an interval of just a couple of months, I decided to start searching in earnest for another dog, a playmate for Fleur. There was no question of a 'replacement', but there was room in our lives for another dog.

Like Fleur and Ci, it would be a rescue dog. It saddens me that shelters everywhere are full to capacity and beyond with lovely dogs who would make great companions while unscrupulous breeders continue to churn out designer cross-breeds of ever more bizarre ancestry. They then charge an absolute fortune for them by giving the 'breed' a silly-sounding name.

The trend started innocently enough, with the Labradoodle. This versatile mix of a poodle and a Labrador was meant to provide an option for a guide dog or disabled assistance dog for people with an allergy to dog hair. Poodles don't moult, so are often tolerated by people with allergies. So it was thought that by crossing them to popular assistance breeds, like the Labrador or Golden Retriever, it would create a non-moulting dog suitable for the job. As is often the way, with crosses, there is no guarantee that some of the offspring won't shed their hair, but the idea was sound.

Now it's just got to the ridiculous stage where all the wannabes want a Cavapoo, a Dane-a-Doodle, a Poozu-Apso, a Chorkie or a Muggins. They're mongrels, people, mongrels. No need to pay thousands for them, just go to your nearest shelter and fork out a couple of hundred. I don't have anything at all against mongrels. I just hate the pretentious way of giving them a silly name to make out they're something else.

Facebook, that dreadful time-waster, can also be a place for hysterical laughter. I was just 'talking' on there to friend and top beta-reader, Emma. We had just seen a post of a dog which was a cross between a German Shepherd, an Akita and a Corgi. We were trying to outdo one another with the silliest name we could suggest for this particular mongrel. I think Emma probably trumped my suggestions of Shepitacor, Shorgita and

Akherdgi with her brilliant German Shitorgi.

I didn't really mind what sort of a dog Fleur and I got, just as long as it was something which would play with Fleur and be sociable. I started looking online at what was currently available at our nearest shelter at Gerzat, not far from Clermont-Ferrand, where I had adopted both Ci and Fleur. They were always hopelessly over-full, eager to rehome any dog they could. They had no time for home visits anyway, but having already let me have two dogs from there, there should be no problem in me having another.

Older dogs are always the hardest to rehome, so I thought it might be nice to get at least a middle-aged one, as long as it still had plenty of play in it. An older dog might also have a steadying effect on Fleur who was still as mad as a box of frogs, despite all my efforts. I didn't mind what breed, although I prefer pastoral breeds, having always had German Shepherds or border collies, plus one collie cross.

Inevitably, living in such a small place, word quickly got round that the mad hippy woman was looking for a dog, so I had several offers, all totally unsuitable. One man came to the gate in his van to say he had a hound which was no good for hunting, if I would like to take it on. After careful questioning, it transpired that 'no good' meant that when she was not rampaging off on her own doing exactly what she wanted to, she was biting people. I thanked him kindly for his generous offer but said that, as I had zero experience of hounds, I would not be the right home for her.

On the website of the refuge at Gerzat, I saw a picture of what looked like a nice border collie bitch, eight years old. The details said she was good with both male and female dogs and had a good basic education, being well behaved both on and off the lead. She was certainly worth going to look at. I took Fleur with me so that, should the dog prove a possible, we could at least introduce the two of them and see if total carnage would result.

I saw the dog in her pen and she certainly seemed nice, calm, friendly and steady. The young man who was showing her to me suggested I bring Fleur in and we would take both dogs to one of the exercise pens to see how they got on. Fleur is always a bit of an uncertainty with others. Despite having the looks of an angel, she really can be a little devil. Surprisingly, there was not much sign of any animosity. I think it was because the other dog was older and had the calm air of self-assurance that maturity can sometimes bring, which defused the situation.

Almost as an aside, the young man said the dog had a mammary tumour and would need to be operated on immediately, but that in view of that, her adoption fee would be much less. He also said the refuge would pay the costs of the operation. I thought it would be a nice thing to do, to take on an older dog which other people might not be queuing up to adopt, so we headed to the reception to fill in the necessary paperwork.

Unfortunately, said young man had not checked with his bosses about who was paying the bills. I would be expected to pay the full costs of the operation, for which a favourable outcome was not guaranteed. Then the story of the dog's origins which they told me were different to what had appeared on the website, where there was also no mention of any tumour. There was a grey area over whether she had been given up for adoption or had been seized from unsuitable owners.

She had come from not far away and this factor worried me. If she had been taken into care from owners who were not happy with the decision, might they not attempt to take her back, if I happened to come across them whilst out walking her one day?

She was a lovely dog. I would have loved to have given her a home. But the way all these things were starting to add up, all I could see was a big hole in my bank balance and no guarantee of a happy ending. Saddened, I had to walk away.

Then, just a couple of days later, one of my Facebook friends posted a photo of a dog on my page. The dog, a black and white border collie, aged about two and called Rosalie, had ridiculously goofy ears and a sad little face. Her eyes were runny, as if she had an infection, and she was totally irresistible.

She was down in the Lot *département* of south-west France, in the Midi-Pyrénées, a long way away. I don't normally approve of shipping dogs all round the country, and certainly not of trans-border transportation, when there are so many in the local refuge. But something about the way she stared at me from the screen of my computer was compelling, so I had to at least find out more.

She was described as extremely nervous, having spent the first two years of her short life chained up. She had no education of any kind and was afraid of things like vacuum cleaners and televisions, which she had never before encountered. But it said she was good natured and eager to please. Above all, the details said the association rehoming her, Last Chance, wanted an experienced border collie home. If she came to join us, she would be my seventh '*bordaire colley*' as the French call them.

I made tentative enquiries, which brought a positive response. I was assured the distance was no object as transport could be arranged to bring her to me, but I would first have to undergo a home inspection to make sure I would be a suitable match for Rosalie and her special needs.

A very nice man came to inspect us and Fleur, as usual, was a total tart, cuddling up to him and schmoozing him as she does with everyone. That, and the thoroughly secure dog-friendly garden, plus me being at home a lot of the time, helped ensure that we passed with flying colours.

All the paperwork sorted and the adoption fee paid, it was arranged that Rosalie would travel up on the twenty-sixth of

December, since Boxing Day is not a Bank Holiday here in France. I would go and pick her up from a café near to a junction on the motorway. By the time she arrived there, she would already have changed vehicles three times, so was likely to be even more nervous.

I barely slept the two nights before her arrival, not just from the excitement of welcoming a new dog into the home, but also from my new life of crime, which merits a chapter of its own later. Fleur and I set off for the meeting, and for what would be our first sight of Rosalie.

After such a long and doubtless confusing journey, with people she had never met before, the poor dog was so bewildered and traumatised she would not get out of the car. She just lay on the floor trembling. The lady who had driven her the latest stretch of her journey, and who was kind and gentle, helped me to pick her up and carry her to my van. We simply plonked her in the back next to Fleur's travel cage, so the two girls could introduce themselves in safety as I drove her back on the final part of her journey to her new forever home.

I have never before encountered such a poor, nervous dog as Rosalie. Everything was scary, even with bouncy, boisterous Fleur to show her around. The first night, she crouched timidly in a corner of the bedroom and peed on the carpet. I couldn't even get a lead on her collar, she was so afraid I was going to grab her. So I didn't even try, I just let her out into the garden and waited for her to come to me.

She quickly became Rosie, it was so much less of a mouthful. Largely by ignoring her, she got brave enough to come and sniff me occasionally as I sat at my desk in the kitchen, working away on my computer. She was considerably underweight and my suspicions about her eyes were quickly confirmed by a vet visit. She had arrived with chronic conjunctivitis and canker in both ears. Treating both of those was not going to be easy in a dog which already avoided being handled.

By the second night, as I got into bed, a black and white shadow glided up onto the bed and curled itself up in a ball by my feet. I hardly dared to move in case I frightened her away. I especially didn't dare stretch my legs out as she was clearly terrified of feet and the prospect of a kick.

Gently, once I switched out the light, I reached out a hand and was rewarded with the briefest of licks. In the words of the lovely Seal song from Batman Forever, I had a kiss from a Rose.

She is still nervous, especially of anything or anyone new. But if you could see her now, comfortably stretched right across the middle of my bed, barely leaving me enough room to get in, let alone to spread out and sleep, you would know that she is now one happy little dog who has very definitely landed on her paws.

She and Fleur are just like human siblings, with occasional snarl-up spats, usually over a bone. Fleur will forever be the bossy one, quick to push Rosie out of the way if she dares to come for a cuddle first.

Their personalities are completely different. Rosie remains a bit of an obsequious Uriah Heap of a dog, who is so grateful for the least kind word or gentle caress. If I'm stroking bossy Miss Fleur and need to stop for whatever reason, she will gently but firmly take hold of my hand in her teeth and put it back on her body. Her message is clear. You can stop stroking me when I say so, not before.

Chapter Eleven
A Life of Crime

Sometimes you hear a story which is so unbelievably cheesy, you know it must be true. No one would go to the trouble of making it up. So you will know straight away, when you read this chapter, that it's gospel. You see, I had a dream …

If you've read *Mother, Was It Worth It?* you will know that my favourite genre of book to read is crime fiction. It's also what I like best on television. I love taking part in the annual reading circle at my local library in Olliergues, especially as each year so far it has been *polars*, crime fiction books.

In the time since I've been here, at least one of the regular members of the reading circle has gone to check in her books at the big library in the sky. But mostly, it's the same people every year. Through it, I've discovered some interesting new authors I might not otherwise have stumbled across.

One year I managed to get to part of the closing ceremony, where we were able to meet three of the authors whose books we had read. I've usually been away that specific weekend, as it's previously fallen on the anniversary of Mother's death.

One book that year was particularly poignant. I was greatly enjoying it as it was an intelligent, suspenseful crime drama, and quite different from others I had read recently. I was just reading the tense terrorist hostage scene in Paris when suddenly, on our television screens, almost the exact same scenario was playing out in real time. The terrible killings at the *Charlie Hebdo* magazine, and subsequent hostage situations, before the perpetrators were finally brought to justice. That really did give me goosebumps.

But with all the different books I read, by different authors, I was getting tired of the lead characters all starting to blend into one with their similarities. The male cops were all tall, heavy drinkers or recovering alcoholics, often chain smokers, rogues, womanisers and rule-benders. The women were so busy showing how ballsy they were in a man's world that, for me, they lost all credibility. I longed to find a policeman who stood out from the crowd without becoming unbelievable.

Then one Christmas Eve, two days before I went to collect Rosie, I had the most amazing dream. I often dream vividly, always in colour. I'm lucky in that I remember most of what I dream on waking, despite my memory not being what it once was. The dream presented me with a brand new copper with a difference, and he came as a complete package.

He was short, only five foot four, he neither drank nor smoked, he was a decent bloke, he didn't need to break the rules because he was good at his job. His team respected him and worked well for him, so his clean-up rate was beyond compare.

He just happened to be called Ted Darling. It's not all that uncommon a surname in the north of England but, of course, it poses endless problems for anyone called that, especially working in the police force. Oh, and almost incidentally, Ted was gay. He lived with an attractive younger man, Trevor, and they had a solid and loving relationship, which of itself stood out from the norm for police officers.

All of this in one dream, you might be wondering? Yes, honestly. I woke up early on Christmas morning, my head still full of Ted. I made myself a cup of rooibos tea, let Fleur out for a widdle, then we went back to bed while I mulled over the finer details of the plot, a large part of which had already formed in my dream.

Once Fleur was walked and had opened her Christmas toy, I sat down in front of the computer and started to write. I barely stopped. Thousands of words flowed out of me with hardly a pause. I've always been a fast writer, throughout my writing career, but I'd never known anything like this before. It was almost how I imagined spirit writing to be. I really felt possessed, as if someone else had taken me over and was using me simply as a vessel to work through. It was at the same time amazing and a bit scary.

The next day, other than walking Fleur and collecting Rosie, almost every other waking minute was spent in front of the computer. For a few days after that, there was no possibility of dog walks. Rosie was still too traumatised by her long journey and the changes in her life so I couldn't even get a lead on her. So I just let the dogs do their own thing in the garden, with the back door open so I could keep an eye on them, while I wrote. And wrote. And wrote.

I was truly like a demented thing, an addict who simply couldn't stop, and I was loving every minute of it. Why had I never thought of trying to write crime before? I couldn't imagine, but I genuinely never had. Now I'd started, though, there was simply no stopping me. I was having so much fun!

Having churned out a huge chunk, I thought I'd better get a bit of feedback early on, in case it was all just the most appalling rubbish, although I did have a feeling it was all right. I sent the first chapter to my friend Jilli in Italy, one of the Three Birds, and anxiously awaited her verdict.

What a relief when it was positive! Our Doris certainly doesn't pull her punches and calls a spade a bloody shovel. But she enthused about Ted, she liked everything about it and kept demanding more. She's a strict alpha-beta reader though, and didn't hesitate to point out any flaws in the plot, anything which needed more explanation or anywhere things needed to be toned down.

As Rosie slowly started to feel more at home and find her

feet, our days would take on a definite pattern. We'd venture out for short walks, so Rosie could get used to her surroundings, then she and Fleur would have the run of the garden while I worked away at the computer. All the time we were out walking, I would be running through plot twists and character interactions in my head, eager to get back to the keyboard to capture them before the ideas were lost.

It's hugely tempting fate to say so, but I have been lucky as a writer in that I hardly ever suffer the dreaded writers' block. Words usually flow fairly effortlessly from my fingers. Admittedly, as a copywriter, writing huge quantities of stuff for online catalogues, my inner gush would sometimes dry up. It would often happen at the sight of yet another pair of earrings which looked to me exactly like the last pair but still needed some 'aspirational' (I still hate that word!) copy to persuade buyers to choose that particular pair.

But generally, the words just flooded out. In the case of Ted Darling, it was a positive torrent. A deluge. A monsoon. Add any metaphor you choose. I just could not stop. What's more, I found I had absolutely no control whatsoever over the serial killer I had created. It even got to the worrying stage of me having mental arguments with the killer over their choice of victims. Even more unnervingly, I wasn't winning.

At the end of each day, I would send the fruit of my labours to Jilli for her feedback. Sometimes, I'd tell her what the killer had in store and she'd join in the argument.

Jilli: Nooooo, you can't let them kill THAT character!

Me: I keep trying to reason with them but they won't listen. Their mind's made up.

Jilli: The readers will never forgive you.

Me: That's what worries me, but I obviously have no say in the matter. They are out of control.

Then, a couple of days later:

Me: Here's today's work. They did it. I tried to stop them, but I couldn't.

Jilli: (wail almost audible all the way from Italy) Nooooo!!

I put on a fair amount of weight over the next few weeks. Between not yet being able to do long walks with Rosie in tow as she was still so nervous, and not wanting to be away from the keyboard, I was turning decidedly podgy. But I was determined to get the book finished and put it out there.

It's not always possible to evaluate your own writing. Some people clearly don't even bother to try to, they just chuck it out regardless. But I wanted this first sortie into crime to be as good as I could possibly make it. It was to be my first venture into published fiction and I wanted it to get at least as good a reception as the travel memoirs have had.

I also needed to find a new pen-name. People are used to me as Tottie Limejuice but somehow, it didn't have quite the right ring to it if I wanted to be taken seriously as a crime writer, which I did. Luckily, I have two first names, if that's not mathematically impossible, and two family names, because of the Luxembourg-British origins. I used my first two initials, L and M and added the Luxembourg family name, Krier (pronounced Kreer, not crier) safe in the knowledge that it was almost certainly unique.

It didn't take me long to finish writing. Then came the longer process of editing, checking, rewriting, and checking again. Finally, on the thirteenth of February 2015 – flying in the face of superstition – the first book, Baby's Got Blue Eyes, was launched.

As an Indie, independently published, writer, contrary to what many people believe, unless you spend your entire time and a substantial budget in marketing, you seldom sell more than a few hundred books. You certainly don't make millions. 'Blue Eyes' did well. It attracted some glowing, genuine reviews. Best of all, people really took to Ted as a character, clearly viewing him as a credible personality.

I was thrilled and flattered at the messages and emails I got, talking almost as if Ted were a real person. My personal favourite was the lady whose husband started drinking green tea after reading that it's Ted's favourite drink. Closely followed by those sending me links to items and pages with a message saying, 'I think Ted would like this, don't you?'

I'd no sooner published the first book than the urge came over me once more and I was back at the keyboard. In less than nine months, I wrote and released three DI Ted Darling books, and I already had the plot for the fourth in my head.

It's the reason I've kept you all waiting so long for this fourth book in the *Sell the Pig* series. You see, the trouble is, I have rather lost my heart to a short, gay detective called Darling.

Chapter Twelve
Calamity Jane

It has to be said, I've never been graceful and ladylike. Despite her paying for me to spend a few years studying for the Royal Academy ballet exams at the Johnson-Podmore School of Dancing in Stockport, where I grew up, my mother always complained that I walked 'like a farmer striding across a ploughed field.'

From the moment I could express an opinion, I wanted to wear trousers and have my hair as short as possible. A real tomboy. While other girls were busy dressing up their Sindy dolls and doing the hair of their Barbies, I was lining my dolls up on the fence and shooting them with my cousin's air rifle. I was always a decent shot, too, even from a young age.

As I get older I seem to be adding clumsiness to my inelegance, in spades. I don't sit up in bed of a morning and wonder what part of my anatomy I can injure next. But despite my best intentions, I always seem to manage to do something stupid.

Whenever I mention on my Facebook page that I'm about to mow the lawn or use stepladders or anything like that, it immediately sparks a chorus of 'Be careful!' from my followers, who clearly know me too well. If I happen to mention power tools will be involved, there is a positive chorus of shrieks of warning.

I do try, I honestly do. I solemnly put on protective clothing and my hefty work boots. Then I forgot to tie a double bow, so the laces come undone, giving me one more trip hazard to contend with.

As soon as the ice and snow arrives, I'm totally neurotic, waiting for the next fall. Not of snow, but of me. Of course, as I get older, I worry about hip fractures, especially out walking boisterous monsters like the collies. I'm at a higher than average risk of osteoporosis, not only because my mother had it, but also because Silly Coeliac stops me absorbing calcium properly. Although touch wood, so far, so good.

I'm sent for osteo-densitometry tests every two years or so, just to check what's going on, and I now have an impressive collection of X-ray shots of my spine and hips. My hips are on the limit of where they should be, but despite the battering it has taken from various horses over the years, including two ruptured cervical discs and a thoracic wedge fracture, my spine is so far doing surprisingly well.

I try to look where I'm putting my feet, remembering Mother's words, saying exactly that phrase, ringing in my ears. Unfortunately I am far too interested in my other mother, Mother Nature, to watch where I'm going. My eye is constantly distracted by the wonders of wildlife.

Oh, wow, is that a short-toed eagle? Splat! Good gracious, that looks like a goshawk flying through the trees. Plop!

Give me a perfectly flat surface, with no signs of a hazard anywhere, and my booted foot will immediately encounter the one and only pebble, tiny, seemingly innocuous, the size of a pea, and start to roll on it. And with all the grace of Dumbo on ice, I will find myself once again down on my bum with my legs in the air.

One time, thinking that our usual footpath would be hazardous because of the autumn invasions of bracken and bramble, the dogs and I scrambled carefully up the bank to the meadow alongside. I knew there were no animals in the field as I'd seen higher up the track that the electric fence was not switched on and had in fact been partly dismantled.

The field had been well grazed down by cattle and was relatively level, smooth, and hazard-free. A much safer bet than the overgrown footpath. I was marching along without a care in the world, marvelling at the autumn colours of the trees. The next moment, thud! Face down in the grass with most of the stuffing knocked out of me. I still have no idea how.

'Oh well,' I thought philosophically, as I lay still for a moment, doing a top to toe self-assessment as I'd been taught on the many first aid courses I've been on, 'at least my face didn't land in one of the fresh cow-pats surrounding me!'

Ci was used to my clumsiness and had even learnt to carry out canine first aid, in his own way. When I went down, he would sometimes, carefully and gently, lie down across me and gently nuzzle my face. Immobilise and reassure the casualty, maintain body temperature. Text book stuff.

Fleur simply accepts it as part of my eccentricity and just waits for me to struggle back to my feet. Poor Rosie is terrified. She clearly associates any sudden foot movement with a kick heading her way, so always leaps out of range as she sees my boots yet again waving in the air.

In recognition of my advancing decrepitude, I got the carpenter who made and installed my new staircase in the grottage to come back and add a handrail. The stairs are quite steep, so now if I do lose my footing and start to fall, I can grab the rail to try to save myself. Although, knowing my luck, I will probably only succeed in pulling it away from the wall and smacking myself over the head with it!

In a previous life I trained and qualified in Risk Assessment and Management, so I do sometimes cast a critical eye around Tottie Towers to see how I can make it more user-friendly.

Attached to my grottage (grotty cottage) is a large barn, much larger, in fact, than the grottage itself. It comprises a cellar, directly under the sitting room, a tractor store, which is actually where I stack my firewood, the large former cowshed, now converted into a dog playpen, and above that, the old hayloft.

When my ship comes in (actually, I think it sank long ago) I have great plans to convert the loft into off-grid living space. I dream of a large, light, airy studio where I can do my writing, looking out directly to the volcanoes in the west, plus a bedroom for me and my dogs. It's way beyond my financial means for the foreseeable future, so it remains a pipe dream.

The loft has tended to be a place for dumping anything and everything. Trip hazards? Too many to count. It's also where the cats, Bibi and HRH the Princess Freddie Mercury, live. I decided to have a concerted effort at tidying it up so there would be fewer obstacles for me to trip over. It took some time, as it involved several trips to the *déchetterie*, the council tip, to get rid of unwanted items, and to recycle the mountains of cardboard boxes left over from moving, since I am hoping that this is my forever home now, as well as Rosie's.

I was beavering away, ridiculously pleased with my efforts, marching to and fro to stack neatly everything which was to stay and leaving much more floor space. As I strode enthusiastically towards the back wall with yet another bed for HRH – like any true royal princess of Siamese descent, she insists on sleeping in a different place each night – the bottom suddenly fell out of my world. Literally.

When I'd first bought the property, the barn roof had been leaking. It was one of the first jobs I had done, to stop the leak before it did too much damage to the structure. Then I'd carefully laid chipboard flooring panels over any areas of the existing plank flooring which had been exposed to the incoming rain.

Unfortunately, I had clearly missed one key area. My large, steel-toe-capped booted foot had gone straight through two narrow planks. My feet may be big but my hips are not. The gap between the cross members of the floor was not wide but plenty wide enough for a snake-hips like me to fall through. It was probably only about a seven-foot drop to the cowshed below but even so, it was enough to break ankles, at least, if not worse.

Painfully, but luckily, although one leg had gone straight through and was dangling in the void above the cowshed, the foot on the back-stride was well and truly wedged, preventing me from falling further. My heel was up behind my hips but my toes, compressed inside the steel-capped boot, were doubled back excruciatingly. They were holding me in place but then, so were the jagged edges of the broken planks. I appeared to be well and truly stuck.

Knowing how accident prone I am, and how much my kind friends worry about me, I am always at pains to carry my mobile phone with me. There's seldom much of a signal, but at least I can try. I had it with me. Safely tucked into the cargo pocket of my work trousers. Halfway down my calf. On the leg which was now dangling, out of my reach, through the hole.

Slowly, carefully, I manage to extricate myself without further damage. I was cut, bruised and battered. I suspected one of my toes was probably broken. But as hospitals seldom do much with broken toes anyway these days, I just carried on limping until it healed itself.

Then there was the time I noticed that the metal arch over the side gate into the garden, with its heavy climbing rose, was in danger of coming down in a high wind. So I climbed up on a chair to secure it. During a high wind. With the probably predictable result that it did fall down, onto my head. I got off lightly, a bump and cut on the forehead, a sore nose, slightly wonky glasses, a stiff neck and some impressive scratches.

Of course, all these accidents don't have a good effect on my long-standing injuries, legacies from my horsey days, especially the spinal ones, which appear to be particularly unforgiving. From time to time, they cause me enough pain and problems to warrant intervention by a 'physioterrorist.'

On one of my trips to Lyon Airport to collect Alex, he noticed immediately that I was wincing with pain at the slightest movement, despite trying not to. I suspected a pulled muscle in my back but at his insistence, I went to see the doctor. It was yet another of the interns my usual doctor helps train. She was extremely thorough and checked everything including my blood pressure, boringly normal, as usual, and my lungs. Whoops, not enough air going into the bottom of one lung. Go and get a X-ray immediately to find out why.

I suspected it was just my pulled muscle not pulling its weight and saving itself, but to humour her, and Alex, I phoned for a hospital appointment at Thiers. Alex came with me, for the ride, and I left him enjoying a coffee while I went to book myself in. Except the helpful lady on reception could find no record of me.

I was convinced I had the date and time right so she kindly rang round local clinics and the next nearest hospital to see if I had the location wrong. Still nothing. Seeing me look slightly crestfallen, she suggested I go to the X-ray department, explain my predicament, and see if they could help me.

I'm not sure how I would have got on at a UK hospital these days without an appointment, but here, they were so kind and helpful. X-ray, no problem, but there was no doctor on duty to give me the results, so they said they would post the films to me to take to my own doctor. The kindly radiographer even helped me on with my coat as she could see I was struggling. As I suspected, there was no sign of anything sinister, so almost certainly a sore muscle just taking it easy.

With all the recent batterings, though, I asked the doctor for a new prescription for some physiotherapy (yes, it really is as easy as that here) and decided to try a new one I had heard good things about, in the nearby town of Ambert. He was an osteopath and physiotherapist, and I knew him by sight, but only at a distance, from the dog training club I attend, where his wife took their young Akita Inu.

Up close, he was absolutely gorgeous. Tall, ripped, dark hair and eyes. The trouble is, it gave me an appalling attack of the stifled giggles as, apart from the eye colour, he was the spitting image of how I had described DI Ted Darling's partner, Trevor, in my new crime books. It didn't help that one day he was wearing a pink polo shirt with crops and sandals, just as I describe Trev as wearing on occasion.

Getting treatment from an osteopath in particular is a bit physically intimate. My poor physio must have wondered what was going on when he was practically lying on top of me, busily crunching various bones back to where they should be, and I was shaking from suppressed laughter, my head filled with images of Trevor.

He was so good at his work that when Alex arrived complaining of pain and numbness down one arm, I took him along to be treated. I gave up one of my slots so he didn't have to wait for an appointment. He was most impressed with the treatment, which considerably relieved his arm but also, by dint of various crunches and cracks around his ribs, helped his breathing a great deal, too.

It's normal in France for people to take long holidays during the summer, and my physio was no exception. There would be a locum on duty while he was away so I would be able to continue the treatment I needed.

What a contrast when I first saw the replacement! Not so much Trevor from my books as Popeye the Sailor Man, the cartoon character, complete with bushy beard. He also wheezed and coughed like Alex on a bad day, so was clearly not the model of good health. He was a good physioterrorist, though. His fingers worked like a concert pianist's, kneading and teasing out the knots in the muscles along my shoulder, bringing enormous relief.

Sadly, I had to stop my course of treatment earlier than I would have liked to, because of all the complications over my health card. I didn't want to find myself with medical bills to pay and no certainty of who was going to cover them, so I would just have to postpone further treatment until my magical *carte vitale* finally arrived.

I popped round to the consulting rooms to settle my bill to date, as that would be covered, because it was for treatment before I found myself without the magic card. 'Trevor' was back from his holidays, so I could continue my treatment with him as soon as things were sorted.

A couple of evenings later I had a phone call from him saying there was a problem with my cheque. I inwardly cringed, as my slight dyscalculia means I am capable of making some appalling blunders when writing out figures, but he hastened to assure me it was not my fault. He had put the cheques on the table in his hall before going out and on his return, he discovered that the Akita Inu, Djoko, had eaten them.

Well, he was at pains to explain that he had managed to recover some pieces – I tried not to dwell on thoughts of their possible provenance – so he could prove to me that the story was true. Would I mind sending another cheque?

That was definitely in the 'you couldn't make it up category'. I assured him I would take him at his word and there was no need to return the recycled pieces of my cheque. I really was suspicious of where they might have been.

Chapter Thirteen
My Tailor is Rich

The teaching of English in French schools has traditionally not been of the highest practical standard over the years. There's no stinting on grammar and vocabulary. But as for speaking it – *sacré bleu*! As a result, I know English learners whose vocabulary is possibly better than that of many English people but who struggle to string together any kind of sentence in spoken English.

Inevitably, as with any foreign language learning, some of the stock phrases students are made to learn have little application in the real world. The traditional one for French students of English was always, 'My tailor is rich.' Not a lot of use in times when hardly anyone, especially round here, has a tailor, and those tailors who are still in business are probably struggling.

It's often been as bad in the past for English students of French who were taught such sublimely useless sentences as *'La souris est en dessous de la table'*, the mouse is under the table, *'le chat est sur la chaise'*, the cat is on the chair and, possibly the hardest to slip into everyday conversation, *'le singe est sur la branche'*, the monkey is on the branch.

The truly brilliant stand-up comedian Eddie Izzard has a side-splittingly funny sketch about his attempts to incorporate these three phrases into daily French usage when visiting the country. If you're interested, especially if you are a fan of his and have not yet seen it, I highly recommend you search for it on YouTube.

I'd really enjoyed running a small English conversation group when I was still living at the Pink House with my brother and mother. I hadn't started up anything similar since moving to the grottage. The house was too small and too hard to find to get much of a group going, and although I'd advertised private lessons, I'd had no takers. They're a notoriously thrifty lot round here and asking even a modest fee for private lessons was greeted with looks of horror.

Our small local town of Olliergues has so much going on it's amazing, much more so than any small town I've ever lived in, in either England or Wales. One of the things it provides is a series of workshops which are free to attend. They cover all sorts of subjects like organic gardening, genealogy, computers, painting.

But in the same way as there is no such thing as a free lunch, they are not free in every sense. They are run on the basis of 'swapsies', which just happens to be my favourite currency. I've never worked on the black, always declared all my earnings, but if I can barter services rather than deal in cash, it's what I always prefer to do.

All those attending any of the workshops are encouraged, in turn, to run one of their own. It could be as basic as a couple of hours showing others how to bake a particular cake or a series of sessions to share their knitting skills. As I'd signed up for the organic gardening course, I went along to see the lady in charge and offered to run a series of six workshops in basic English, proudly waving my TEFL certificate, Teaching English as a Foreign Language.

I offered six as a sort of starter pack, a survival guide, for beginners and others lacking in confidence, so they could get by in English when they needed to. Basic but invaluable stuff for travelling, like being able to spell your own name correctly, give telephone numbers in English format, rather than French, and ask for help where needed.

French numbers still stump me, because I struggle with numbers in any language. The French give their phone numbers in an entirely different way to the English, grouped into a series of two-digit numbers. I'm not giving you mine, but here's an example which is similar. I can remember my mother's phone number in England which would always be given in the English format: oh-one-six-one, four-eight-three, double-five-eight-three. In French format, that would be oh-one, sixty-four, forty-eight, thirty-five, fifty-eight, three, or possibly five hundred and eighty three. Confused? I always am!

As an aside, a word here on French telephone directories, for those who have not yet experienced them. They differ from English ones in an important way. Let's suppose you are in England, or Wales. Wales is a good example. You're in the Swansea area and you want to contact an old friend, whose phone number you have mislaid, so you pick up the telephone directory.

Unfortunately, said friend has the most common Welsh surname of all, Jones. To make matters worse, his name is Dai, just as common. Worse still, you don't know if Dai is his first or middle name, as people in Wales are often known by their middle name.

You know he lives in the area somewhere but not exactly where. You then have to trawl through pages and pages of D. Jones's in the entire Swansea area to see if you can find one who might possibly be your friend. Not very practical, you might think. So would you fare any better in France?

Here the directory is laid out not by name but by commune, that being a town and its satellite villages, then under each of those headings, the listing is alphabetical in name order. So, let's say you find yourself in this *département*, 63, the Puy-de-Dôme, trying to find your friend Monsieur Martin who, unluckily for you, has the most common French surname and an equally popular first name, Louis.

This time, you need to know the commune in which he lives in order to find his number. You may even know the village he's in, but unless you happen to know what commune it comes under, you have a lot of Google searching ahead of you before you can begin to use the directory.

We had great fun debating in the workshop which country's system is better, since there are clearly major drawbacks with both. Apparently, we are no longer going to have paper phone books at all in the future here. The assumption is that everyone has access to the Internet, or to someone else who does. It should save a few trees, but there may be trouble ahead. I'm certainly going to hang on to my old ones, just in case.

I thought my sessions, which were intended to be 'English made easy', would be nice and relaxed and informal, but in fact it was rather like being back in Further Education, as I once was. I had to produce lesson plans and schemes of work, and there were frequent appraisal meetings to see how it was all going. Despite all that, the actual workshops were a lot of fun.

There was a good turnout for my first session and there were only two drop-outs over the series of six, which was a good result. As always, I kept it light-hearted, lots of laughter amongst the learning, and above all, there was cake.

The first week, I took in some shortbread, since it's a nicely traditional British recipe, very easy to make. I make it with rice flour, which I can eat and which gives a wonderful texture. So when we paused for a coffee break, we all munched biscuits together, then I gave my students the recipe and we worked through it in English. The idea behind the workshops was a sharing of skills, so I hoped that my students would spread their new shortbread-making skills around the area.

I only committed to six workshops because I had so many projects in my head at once that I wasn't sure I could keep up the standard if I offered to do more. As well as writing the crime and finishing the travel memoirs, I had also branched out into children's fiction for the first time.

An English friend, Avril, from Olliergues, also a TEFL teacher, was going to take over my learners after my six week course was up. She was also running a more advanced group, into which some of my fledglings could fly when they felt themselves to be ready.

My students were great. There was the usual mix. The serious ones who brought in self-inflicted written homework every week to be checked. The class comedian who wanted to learn every slang word for cannabis and tried to inject one or other into any sentence. Those clearly just looking for a bit of company of an afternoon.

Their reasons for attending were as varied. Some just wanted to stretch themselves with a new language. Others felt they had never got to grips with English at school and wanted to try again. A few wanted to learn because English is so much the language of the Internet and all things computer that they found themselves struggling without a better grasp.

One of the advantages of the room we were allocated to hold the workshops in was that it housed the young men of the equivalent of the River Board here. These were the people who cleaned and preserved waterways and banks and carried out maintenance of open spaces.

Because my workshop was on a Friday afternoon when they finished early, we would often find dishy young men wandering about, peeling off their outdoor wear to dry it out on the various radiators around the building, where the temperature was always cranked up high for just that reason.

I loved the sessions I held. I wished I had time to do more but the simple fact is, I didn't. Apart from the writing, I had other projects in mind, like Tottie's Tours, another of my crazy ideas.

But I did become great friends with one of my former pupils and we still meet up at least once a week. Which one? The class comedian, of course!

Some expats claim it's hard to make friends with the French, insisting that they are cold and closed. I never have a large circle of friends, wherever I hang my hat. But I now count a handful of Auvergnats amongst my close friends and I find they have opened their homes and their hearts to me, to give me a friendship which I cherish.

My former student, Domi, expressed an interest in reading my crime books, quite a challenge since they were not written with English learners in mind. So together we work through them, large dictionary in hand, and she is making amazing progress.

I never realised quite how much slang and northern colloquial English I used in writing them until we began our mammoth task. She's gobbled up some of the slang words with evident delight, although I'm not sure I should be teaching her words like 'piss off', 'dickhead' and 'bollocks'!

Chapter Fourteen
Tottie's Tours

When you live in a beautiful area, it's natural to want to share it with people. Up to a point. I love having visitors, showing them round all the interesting sites, taking them to sample the wonderful food. But I have to confess, I rather enjoying waving them off at the end of their stay – until the next time.

I'd hate to have a permanent influx of incomers to the area, although I know the comparatively short tourist season brings in valuable revenue for many people. A big part of the charm, though, is the low population and vast open space. There are more cows than people around here. It's not for nothing that the Auvergne recently featured as one of the top ten destinations on Lonely Planet.

One thing visitors often remark on is how clean everywhere is. The streets, the countryside. There is litter, of course, although nothing remotely like parts of the UK. There's even some graffiti about, though mostly in the towns. One local wag did once shin up a sign post and add the word 'blow' in front of the place name Job, although I suspect the wit was lost on much of the local population, who don't speak English.

As I was walking across the market square just this morning, I saw where someone had dropped their newly-purchased ripe melon and it reminded me of something else I've not yet seen around here. Something which looks not dissimilar to splattered melon, usually found outside pub doorways.

When I lived with my brother in Wales for six months, awaiting the move out to France, his house, situated as it was on a corner of a busy street between several pubs, was the evening meeting place for the Kidwelly formation vomiting team, it seemed. Delightful! But although there is, of course, alcohol abuse here as everywhere, I tend to see much less evidence of it, which is all to the good.

Not that I am remotely comparing myself to the likes of Peter Mayle and his 'Year in Provence', but I do know that people are often fascinated by the idea of going to see where books are set. I've not yet had any readers turn up unannounced on my doorstep, but it would be easy enough to do. So the idea of Tottie's Tours was born.

I decided to put together a sort of package tour, where people could come and discover the area and, if they wished to, meet me and my dogs. The idea would be based round a one-week visit and would include conducted tours by me of some of the places mentioned in the *Sell the Pig* books, plus some free time to go off exploring, armed with maps and directions which I would provide.

Olliergues would definitely be on the agenda. It's a quirky and interesting little town, with its sometimes steep cobbled streets. Being on an oxbow on the river, it's not always straightforward to walk around, as it's not always readily obvious which is the shorter route from one point to another, because of the curves and contours. I'd done the guided tour of the town myself several times when I was brushing up my French for the exam necessary for my citizenship examination, so I was getting adept at showing people around.

There are so many things to see in this area that it was harder to decide what to leave out rather than what to include for my Tour proposal. I put together an itinerary, tried bits of it out on various visitors, and thought it could work. I was planning on small groups of four to six and had the idea of putting them up in a *gîte*, the furnished holiday lets beloved of the French.

I've stayed in some excellent ones with Alex, Jill and my other visitors. They're great value, ideal for a relaxed holiday, especially for me, taking my dogs everywhere with me. For the price of a cheap hotel room you get a cosy place to stay with two or three bedrooms, sometimes more, a fully equipped kitchen and dining area, seating space, a shower and loo and often an outside terrace for sitting out enjoying the sunshine.

With reasonably cheap flights from the UK either direct to Clermont-Ferrand or coming via Paris, I thought it would make an enjoyable and affordable holiday. I hadn't realised how much people these days are obsessed with an en suite bathroom. They're not even all that common in homes in this area. Most French people seem to be capable of staggering a couple of yards along a landing to use the facilities. In fact even the phrase '*en suite*' for an attached bathroom has no meaning in French, it's a British invention.

I'm used to holidays sharing with complete strangers, from all the trail-riding best friend Jill and I have done over the years. We've shared a leaking tent in the American Rockies and a bivouac in Corsica. I've slept in a tent in the Canadian Rockies with six strangers and only bears and wolves for neighbours. Our washing facilities have sometimes been a river so chilly we've needed to keep our T-shirts on while we washed. And as for sanitation! Our kindly trail cook in the States, when we asked about facilities, simply said, 'Honey, you take a shovel, go find a tree and you squat!'

But it seems that today's traveller likes home comforts above adventure, prefers their own space and above all, their own bathroom, to the chance of meeting new people.

Totties' Tours didn't get into full swing this year. Undaunted, I am relaunching the whole idea in 2016, with a much broader selection of accommodation choices, from cheap and cheerful up to luxury B&B. I already have enquiries for next year and some are so intriguing they will doubtless be material for a book of their own, particularly the coven of witches wanting to come on motorbikes. I kid you not.

In the meantime the search is on to find even more interesting sights to show the intrepid Totties' Tourers, and Domi has been a great help in taking me to places I'd not yet discovered.

She knows how intrigued I am by folklore and how I love to commune with nature, so she promised to take me to a special place. She would tell me only that one thing we were going to see on the visit was the Devil's Tree.

We went in her car, leaving the dogs behind, and it was not far to our first stop. She was particularly mysterious about this site, saying only that it had to be felt, not described. We left the car at the roadside and walked up a rough track a short distance, until we came to a small clearing in the woods. There was a standing stone, a cross. Domi said nothing, just left me to make of it what I would.

I was drawn to the stone, felt compelled to put my hand against it and hold it there. The cold granite seem to warm up at the contact. Energy field? Portal? Whatever your beliefs, something was sending warmth into my body. It could not have been simply stored heat from the sun. The stone was in dappled shade, and it clearly was for much of the day. It had felt cold to the touch initially.

I turned my back to lean against it, enjoying the warmth that produced. It was still and quiet in the clearing, with barely a bird calling. I could feel eyes watching me from the trees. Not animals, not people. I have no rational explanation. It was not unlike what I had felt at the national Maquis memorial at Mont Mouchet, though this time I could only sense, not see, the presence of something or someone.

From there we walked a short way back down the track, then branched off into the trees. There, on a mossy knoll, a huge round boulder was balanced precariously, a remnant of former volcanic activity. Here the feeling was completely different. The vibes were all of gaiety and feasting. I half expected to see nymphs, dryads and fawns capering in the dappled sunlight. Had Mr Tumnus appeared, complete with woolly scarf wound round his neck, I would not have been surprised.

Then it was back into the car to visit the Devil's Tree, a short drive away. I'm not going to say too much about it here, so as not to spoil the visit for any who choose to come to the Auvergne, either on Tottie's Tours or independently. Suffice it to say that the tree itself is a remarkable sight, and it has next to it a sign which recounts the history of what happened when the Devil passed that way on his black horse. I can't tell you any more here. It might give you nightmares – pun intended!

A fascinating place to visit, but sadly not physically possible to get my friend Alex there. The walk is not long but it would be beyond his limits on foot, and too rough to even contemplate taking the wheelchair. And I always try to take Alex wherever it's humanly possible. Even if sometimes I get a bit carried away by my own optimism.

The Auvergne is situated fairly centrally in France and my area, the Livradois-Forez, sits on its eastern edge, bordering the next region of Rhône-Alpes. There is currently great trepidation and anticipation here as our region is about to be combined with that one in a major boundary change. Although we are geographical neighbours, it's a bit like asking Tyneside to merge with the Home Counties. Goodness knows how it will turn out.

The Forez mountains, close to where I live, form the current boundary between our two regions. The highest point is near the Col du Béal, at Pierre sur Haute. My interest in the neighbouring region is usually confined to walking up to the summit and peering across at it, always hoping to get a glimpse of Mont Blanc, which is visible from there, usually on cold frosty days. Although of course I have been adventurous enough to stray over the line on a few occasions.

There is a military installation on the summit of the mountains, with a tarmac road up to it, which is restricted to military vehicles. It's a pleasant cross-country walk of about five kilometres to get to the top without using the road, though with a few steep climbs, totally impossible for Alex. But the road surface is fine for a wheelchair and although it's steep in parts, I thought I should at least be able to push him part of the way along it, for the views, so he could take some photos.

Alex pointed out the obvious insanity of factors such as him weighing seventeen stone and me little more than nine. Also the fact that I still had the torn muscle in my back which was preventing me from breathing to full capacity. But my motto these days is, 'If not now, when?' We're both in our sixties already so we're hardly likely to get any fitter which each approaching year.

There's an Irish folk song with a marvellous line about getting satisfaction from thinking 'at least I tried.' That's how I was feeling. Alex could walk short distances on the flat, so I could rest then, and save my energy for the big push on the inclines. So with Fleur's lead firmly tied to my waist to leave my hands free, as this was the period between losing Ci and getting Rosie, off we set on our big, ambitious adventure.

I managed to push for nearly two kilometres, with lots of stops along the way, on the pretence of them being photo opportunities. We were trundling along our way, Alex wheeling for all he was worth, me pushing as hard as I could on one and a half lungs, when a swish new estate car overtook us, continued for a good few metres then stopped and backed down towards us.

The smart young couple inside the equally smart and shiny car asked if we would like a lift to the top. Is the Pope a Catholic? Or, as my befuddled mother once said, 'can the pope swim?' I pointed out that we did have a hairy and by now somewhat muddy dog but they were kindness itself, saying we were all welcome, mud, hairs and all. Although I spoke to them in French, they both spoke excellent English to Alex.

The nice young man folded the wheelchair and stowed it in the boot while Alex and I got in. We sat on beautiful and doubtless expensive leather seats, Fleur firmly squashed between my feet so she couldn't do her usual trick of leaping about barking and slobbering all over the windows. Then we were whisked away right up to the top, at the point where the road finished.

The view from the summit was magnificent, even if we couldn't quite see as far as Mont Blanc. Alex took dozens of photos from the vantage point, before we set off on our way back down. Funnily enough, the effort of holding back the chair and its passenger, even with him using his hands to block the wheels as much as possible, was even more painful for my back then going up had been.

But we did it. Another adventure ticked off, another challenge confronted and surmounted. If not now, when?

Chapter Fifteen
Hello 21st Century

Not much more than ten years ago, I had never touched a computer in my life. I'm from an older generation. We simply did not have them back in my day. They were the stuff of science fiction. Give me an electric typewriter, though, and I could rattle away at an impressive rate, and all without looking at the keyboard.

I was taught proper touch-typing, a tea-towel covering my hands, music playing in the background, while I and the rest of my Commerce class at Stockport College, tapped out 'a s d f j k l ;' in time to the music, before graduating to rattling off such useful sentences as ' The quick brown fox jumps over the lazy dog'. My party piece was always that I could type faster than a telex machine could send. Younger readers won't even know what a telex machine is, of course.

When I became a freelance copywriter, at the turn of the millennium, I had to learn computer skills on the job, as all the work I got was via email. It was a massive learning curve, but I more or less got there.

These days, many of us have become so used to the wonders of the Internet that we barely give it a second thought. I spend a vast amount of time connected to the web, chatting on social media, keeping in touch with friends via email and researching for my books.

It's amazing to what degree most of us have become used

to and dependent on it. For example, I don't have a landline, just an Internet phone, because it works out much cheaper. But when we get our not infrequent thunderstorms, I have to unplug the Livebox router to save it from lightning strike, which means no phone and no Internet.

I can remember the frustrating days of dial-up connections, when it used to take literally hours to open most things. Now we have broadband, of a sort, although that is sometimes as much use as a piece of wet string, but at least it's there. We tend nowadays to take for granted that everywhere we go will have an Internet connection, although that's not always the case.

On our travels round the Auvergne, I was determined to take Alex to see at least one of the designated *Plus Beaux Villages de France*, Most Beautiful Villages of France, of which the Auvergne has eleven of the country's one hundred and fifty-seven. So far I'd only managed to show him Lavaudieu, in the Haute-Loire, from a distance since, like many of them, it's traffic-free, except for residents, and the road up to it is steep and not exactly wheelchair-friendly.

Since the Cantal *département* of the Auvergne has lots of interesting places to visit, and I knew at least one of its *Plus Beaux Villages* would be accessible to us, I decided to take Alex there for a couple of days on his visit in May one year. So far he has tried always to come in a different month each time so he can see the different seasons and how they impact on the flora and fauna. The day I set off to pick him up from Lyon, I heard the first golden oriole, returning for the summer.

Since moving here, my diary is full of such entries. The first cuckoo, (April 2nd, 2013, April 1st 2014), the return of the swallows, as well as their departures, when the evenings start to draw in once more and it's time for us to brace ourselves for whatever winter has planned. Even weather forecasters don't really profess to forecast Auvergnat weather, for which capricious doesn't come close to describing it.

Anyone coming on Tottie's Tours and asking what to wear will get my stock answer: 'the only predictable thing about the Auvergne's weather is its unpredictability.' We quite often see all seasons in one day. Just yesterday, without a hint of it in the forecast, there was a sudden tremendous flash of lightning, alarmingly close to my house, followed almost immediately by a huge crack of thunder. I was outside in the garden at the time. I usually love watching storms but this was so sudden, and so close, I very nearly joined Fleur in the sanctuary she hides in under my desk.

I'd picked Salers for the visit to the Cantal with Alex, and had found online a nice municipal camping site, with comfortable chalets at an affordable price. Salers is one of the *Plus Beaux Villages* and the region is the birthplace of the glorious red cows, with their rich mahogany coats and vast, lyre-shaped horns, as well as the excellent cheese of the same name.

The Massif du Cantal is also import geologically as it is the largest stratovolcano in Europe, in terms of surface area. Volcanic activity in the area began thirteen million years ago, with the last major eruptions some two million years ago. One of the plus points of the area for us is that there is a road which goes over the top of the Puy Mary, close to its summit, at more than seventeen hundred metres, with some stunning views. A perfect photo opportunity for Alex, and one to which I could get him with relative ease.

Jill and I had tried to go up over Puy Mary on our trip round the Auvergne when I was first thinking about the area as a future home, but had found the summit blocked by snow and the road closed. I vaguely remembered us parking near to an *auberge* and going for a bracing walk in the snow, which was above our knees in places.

I found what I thought was the right road on the map, heading towards Salers, and off we set intrepidly in my little yellow van, with the hippy stickers all over it. I love the mountains. Love looking at them, love walking in them. I'm not so good at driving in them, for some reason. The drops give me vertigo when on wheels, even in places I can happily walk.

To make matters worse, we were on the right road, but going in the opposite direction to the way I'd been before, which meant we were coming up the steeper side, with some interesting drops.

Alex was loving it, his camera constantly clicking, as he kept up a running commentary.

'Wow, look down there, that's amazing!'

Click, click, click.

'I can't look down there because I have my eyes closed.'

'You can't drive with your eyes closed!'

Suddenly no more clicking.

'Well, I'm managing quite well. Just tell me if there's anything coming the opposite way. And stop telling me to look down.'

We made it, unscathed, to the summit, where I even managed to find a place to pull over in the van while Alex took some more photos. We stopped at the *auberge*, not far down the other side from the summit, where hot drinks were in order as the wind was decidedly chilly, then on to the camp-site to find our appointed chalet.

I went to reception to collect the keys and asked, almost in passing, for the code to access the wi-fi, or as it's pronounced here, the 'wee-fee'. I gaped at the man in astonishment when he informed me there was none. What were we to do? Alex and I are a pair of social media addicts, forever posting photos and stuff about our various visits. How would we cope? There wasn't even much of a signal for Alex's posh phone, which is capable of posting his photos to Facebook by some magical means which is totally beyond my comprehension.

Our only hope of contact with the outside world would be the free wi-fi at local libraries or Internet cafés. Except May is a month with a lot of *jours fériés*, Bank Holidays, in it. May 1st, Labour Day. May 8th, VE Day, Victory in Europe, when we'd been to the commemorative ceremony at the war memorial in Olliergues. May 14th, Ascension Day, May 25th, Whitsuntide, despite France being a secular country. And on these public holidays, the libraries would be closed. We were there for Whitsuntide. We'd just have to manage with books to read and each other to talk to.

Our chalet was comfortable and well equipped, so we made ourselves at home and sat out on the terrace to eat our evening meal. A Bernese Mountain Dog appeared and tried to make friends with Fleur and Rosie. Fleur is a rabid racist and for some reason hates Swiss dogs with a particular passion, so we had to keep persuading him to depart with a few strategic shots from a water pistol.

The next day we went to look at Most Beautiful Villages. Salers itself is certainly beautiful but, even early in the season, it was crowded. It was Rosie's first experience of one of our trips away, Fleur, of course, being an old hand at it. So many crowds were a bit of a challenge to a nervous dog like her but as usual, we met with understanding and patience from French people who wanted to make friends with her but understood her fears.

We decided to shop for a picnic and find somewhere a bit quieter, so we headed for another Most Beautiful Village, not far away, Tournemire. We had to leave the van at the edge of the village and take the wheelchair for Alex but it was beautifully quiet after Salers, with some wonderful views and plenty of photo opportunities.

Once again it was a challenge to my puny muscles as there were lots of ups and downs to be tackled with the chair. It was well worth it, though. A beautifully sunny day made it ideal to sit and rest in a pretty small square. All the road names there were in French as well as the Auvergnat language, a dialect of Occitan. Hence names such as *Place de l'Église*, Church

Square, which was also written as *Plaça de la Glèisa*.

We managed to find an Internet café on our travels, where we stopped for coffees and eagerly asked for the wi-fi access code. The lady in charge was apologetic and said the system was flaky at the best of times and was currently unreliable. We tried. Nothing. Even in a backwater like this, we have become used to taking Internet access for granted, so we were surprised to find none at all for our entire mini-break.

Not long after our return from the Cantal, when I was walking the dogs in the woods near the grottage, I saw vans and workmen, installing manholes and poking cables down them, heading in the direction of my house. Then I saw the magic words on the side of one of the vans. Fibre optic!

Could it be? Was tiny little Le Mas about to get acquainted with the 21st century? I asked one of the workmen and he confirmed that they were indeed installing fibre optic cable.

Soon after, I rushed round to our *mairie* to find out what was going on and whether or not all of us would be able to connect up to this miracle of modernity. The man on duty behind the desk was highly amused by my evident excitement and use of the word miracle. It transpired that the cable was being installed to furnish the tourist office for the regional nature park in which we are situated, a short distance lower down in the valley below my house.

The *Maison du Parc* has lots going on, film shows, book readings and all manner of other activities, for which they desperately needed a better Internet connection. Since the heavy unexpected snows one year, which took down miles of phoneline, our piece of wet string had been even slower and more precarious than ever, so they were updating with fibre optic. The cable would pass right by my grottage and, I was informed, anyone who wished to could be connected to the network. In about two or three months time.

Of course, those are Auvergnat months because, six months on, there is still no sign of any connection being offered. So we plod along with our wet string, slow connections, dropping out and the associated frustrations. But one day, soon, we too may join the 21st century.

Chapter Sixteen
Bang, Bang!

Before you all rush to sell up in the UK and move to rural France after reading the books, let me tell you about one of its biggest drawbacks. The hunting season. It begins in September and goes on until February, although sometimes an extension is granted.

Hunting days vary for different places. Here, it tends to be Thursday, Saturday and Sunday, although it's not unusual to hear the odd gun banging away on intervening days as well. Or nights, which isn't actually allowed. It's somewhat disconcerting to be out in the garden with the dogs after dark and to hear the crack of a rifle, seemingly perilously close, without being able to see who's shooting. So how the heck can they see what they're shooting at?

What do they hunt? Round here it's wild boar, deer, foxes, ducks, and lots more, plus anyone foolish enough to be out in their line of fire. Theoretically, everyone shooting these days has to wear fluorescent orange gear to avoid getting themselves shot, but still every year, there are accidental human fatalities on the shoots.

This being France, an awful lot of alcohol is involved in the hunting get-togethers, so sometimes the aim is not quite as true once they start shooting, especially after lunch. Or maybe it's just a clever way of settling old scores, in the guise of an accident. Who knows? There have even been cases of hounds shooting their owners by knocking over a loaded gun.

I always carry a fetching bright orange beanie in my bag of equipment for taking on dog walks. That way if the hunters should happen to be in an area where I'm not expecting them, I can at least put that on to make myself more obvious.

Even in the rural areas, hunting is highly controversial. I was surprised, in my English workshops, when not one of the eight students in the room was in favour of it. I often encounter French people who are vehemently opposed. Yet it still goes on. There has been a move recently to get it banned on Sundays. Not for religious reasons, just so that families can have one day of walking in the woods at weekends without getting peppered with shot.

When the elections for our local council took place, the results were interesting. There were two groups of candidates standing, one of which was predominantly the hunters. I don't know whether it was their politics or their pastimes which influenced the vote. I do know they were soundly thrashed and none of them was elected.

Arguably, numbers of some species do need to be controlled, especially now the larger predators are out of the equation, as they are here. There have been moves to reintroduce wolves in some areas, strongly opposed by farmers, and there are rumours of one or two wolves moving back into the Cantal *département* of the Auvergne.

Although I often see recent traces of wild boar in the woods where I walk the dogs daily, I've never yet seen one in the flesh here, though I have elsewhere. I understand and accept they can cause great damage to crops, and I've seen for myself how they get clever enough to beat even electric fencing around fodder maize, for instance. I've seen where they've managed to pull down a maize plant across the wire, shorting out the circuit and letting them in to eat their fill.

I often see deer, usually roe deer, on my walks, and always stop to marvel at their shy beauty. I hate to see them fleeing in terror before the hounds and guns of the hunters. I always wear the bear bells I brought back from Canada whenever I walk during hunting season. It's partly to alert the hunters to my presence, so they don't shoot me, but also to warn the deer and other wildlife that it's time they moved. I also sing loudly as I walk along, which tends to scare anything away.

It's surprising how much of an impact the brief hunting season has on the life of me and the dogs. We like to go to our dog training classes every week but once the hunting starts, there's no point even taking Fleur when the classes are held up at Fournols. The hunters are always out and about there and she has incredibly good hearing. She knows when hounds or guns are within a huge radius and I can't get any work out of her at all. She just wants to hide and tremble.

As for going out for walks here, or even prising Fleur out into the garden – forget about it. I swear that she also has an uncanny ability to know when 4x4s or white vans driving past the house are going hunting or not. We have lots of them here anyway, but as soon as they appear in hunting season, she goes and hides under my desk in the kitchen and can only be coaxed out for food.

The cats, too, have to be confined to barracks whenever the hunters are around. Little Bibi, the black and white one, is pretty streetwise, and also easy to identify as a cat. HRH the Princess Freddie Mercury, with her darker, half Siamese colouring, could easily pass for a small fox, as some of the foxes round here are dark-furred. So I tend to keep them shut in the barn on hunting days, for their own safety, which is not popular.

I have a fiendish plan to construct something like a fruit cage around the balcony to the hay loft, so I can keep the cats in there on when necessary, thus allowing them at least some sunshine to bask in. My scheme involves stepladders, above a drop, electric power tools, a rampant climbing rose, and me – what could possibly go wrong?

Trying to go on one of my wild camping adventures in hunting season is particularly perilous as, if I'm not careful, I might find myself as the prey.

One chilly winter's night I decided it might be rather fun to go and wild camp in the van near to the top of the Col du Béal. There's no wild camping allowed at the summit itself, because of the varied and fragile flora and fauna. In any event, I did a quick recce up there for a suitable overnight pitch and found the doors of my van froze shut in minutes, so clearly that was not my most sensible idea.

So I drove lower down, with the dogs in the van, into the heavily wooded lower slopes. I was with Ci and Fleur, on this occasion. But every time I thought I had found a decent pitch and was settling down to read my book in peace, hunters would appear, either on foot or in their 4x4s. Deciding discretion was the better part of valour, I had to move on again.

Since losing Ci, I had rather lost my confidence for wild camping. Ci would, without a doubt have protected me with his life, should the need have arisen. No one, man nor beast, was allowed to approach his beloved *maitresse* without the threat of being torn limb from limb and then consumed. Small he may have been, but in protection mode, he was a formidable sight to behold.

Blonde and beautiful Fleur is a completely different character. With dogs, she will happily bark racist abuse at any dog, especially Swiss or German breeds. She could, as they say, start a fight in an empty room. She's totally undeterred by size and will attack anything she takes a dislike to, even, on one occasion, picking a fight with a Newfoundland twice her size and three times her weight because it looked at her the wrong way.

But people? People are for licking, snogging, cuddling, smooching and making eyes at, in Fleur's book. I wouldn't put any faith in her protecting me. I am never far from my SAS knife, a gift from the extremely unsuitable character with whom I once had a torrid affair, and I would, if necessary, wield it in my defence. But Fleur, for close protection work? I'd be better off with HRH. At least her glacial blue stare can freeze her enemies on the spot.

For the Winter Solstice after Ci's sudden departure, I wanted to mark it in some way, so decided to try to find a camp-site which was open all year round. There are not many people mad enough to go camping in the Auvergne once winter sets in. Those who do tend to be in winterised caravans or motorhomes, so with my little tent, I can usually find a quiet corner of a site with no near neighbours.

I found a site via the Internet, which was not too far away, and emailed them to check they would be open for one mad person and a dog in a tent for one night, which they confirmed. When I arrived, on the appointed day, although the site was open, there was no sign of anyone around.

Fleur and I went for a walk in the woods while we waited. I was, as ever, keen to get the tent up in plenty of time before it got dark. Even with my trusty 2-second instant-pitch Quechua tent, I like to be sorted and settled.

After our walk, there was still no one to ask where to pitch and when I checked, the sanitation block, with the loos and showers, was firmly locked up for the winter. It wasn't looking hopeful. It was a Dutch-owned site and it has to be said, I haven't had a lot of luck with those.

Eventually I tracked down the owner, who looked surprised to see me, despite my email. He had been busily pruning trees around the site but found me a quiet corner with not too many fallen branches on it and promised faithfully to open one loo and a shower for me, although, in fact, he completely forgot to do so. Because he was not fully prepared, he gave me a cheap deal for the night.

With the lack of sanitation, it was quite like wild camping. It never bothers me, I'm quite used to it. I just behave like a bear, and we all know what they do in the woods. I had plenty of water and my trusty gas and spirit stoves for heating it up, so I could wash and have hot drinks.

My reward for our adventure was the most spectacular view of the sun setting behind the chain of volcanoes directly opposite our tent, in the sparkling frost.

It was cold enough in the night for the tent to freeze hard, but Fleur and I were as snug as bugs inside, me in my sleeping bag, her cuddled up in the small of my back with an extra layer thrown over the top of both of us.

It was only a few days after that that Rosie came into our lives and had to learn all about this strange camping lark her new owner and big sister Fleur seemed so keen on. To begin with, she was absolutely terrified of the idea of going into a tent. Confined spaces seemed to cause her a lot of anxiety, and were obviously linked to bad experiences in her short life.

As I wanted her to join us to celebrate the Summer Solstice in a tent, as I usually do, I had to pitch the tent in the garden at the grottage to get her used to it. I then spent a lot of time coaxing her into it with titbits, then encouraging her to lie down and stay in it, while seasoned camper Fleur cuddled up to me and I read a book. Gradually she got used to the strange idea and we graduated to sleeping in it for the night.

Then the big adventure. I'd asked to be able to use the dog training field up at Fournols for the night. It was ideal because, although it appeared to be in the middle of a forest miles from anywhere, in fact our dog trainer's house was just a hundred yards away down the road, but out of sight.

It would be like wild camping, though not quite in the wilds. Rosie clearly thought me completely mad when, after her training class, when the other dogs departed, we stayed behind. What's more, we put up that funny kennel thing she'd learned to sleep in, then all crawled inside it to sleep.

Welcome to your crazy, but very loving, new home, Rosie.

Chapter Seventeen
It's a Dog's Life!

My dogs are a hugely important part of my life. It's no exaggeration to say that they are the centre of my universe. I've lived without human company for about thirty years now, apart from the brief interlude spent with my mother and brother. For me, it really is a case of 'love me, love my dogs.'

Friends who come to visit are well aware that my life is largely ruled by my dogs. Time away from the house is always restricted, so they are not left alone too long. Journeys away with them have to be, of necessity, to dog-friendly destinations. That aspect is much easier in France than in parts of the UK as dogs are widely welcomed in hotels, on camp-sites and in self-catering accommodation.

Having survived one encounter with Jilli, from Italy, also known as Doris Bird, I was quite keen to meet up with her again, which may come as a surprise to those who know her. I particularly wanted to visit her in Italy as I've only been to the country once and that was many years ago. Alex was keen to come too, as he's never been there.

After the success of our joint book, Take Three Birds, Jilli and I were looking at ideas for a sequel. Because of the way it was written, it would have to be done from a different angle, with a change to the central characters, as the readers already knew a lot of their back-stories. We quite liked the idea of something like Two Birds and an Old Bloke, featuring Alex, but it was still only a draft idea. Possibly even a daft idea.

It's a long old drive from here to Jilli's place in the Emilia-Romagna region, south of Tuscany. It had taken Doris Bird and Farmer Bird the best part of twelve hours to get here, as they had got spectacularly lost on the way. It shouldn't be more than about an eight-hour drive, but travelling with dogs on board, we would clearly have to make frequent stops.

For Alex's spring visit in 2015, we had planned a trip to the Vercors Massif, between Lyon and Grenoble, in the Rhône-Alpes region. As this would already put us well on our way to Italy, we decided to combine the two trips. We planned to spend a couple of days in the Vercors, a region of spectacular plateaux and mountains, steeped in wartime history as a Maquis stronghold. From there we'd cross the border into Italy to go and spend a couple of day with Jilli. That way, the dogs could come with us.

People tell me I spoil my dogs. Of course I do! They're my family, my babies. Why wouldn't I? Some people, who don't know me all that well, suggest I should just put them in kennels and go off doing whatever I want without them. Presumably these same people put their children in a home when they go away. To me, it's not dissimilar.

I know there are some good kennels. I've recently discovered one near to here which makes an excellent day crèche for my monsters, if I want to go out for the day to somewhere not dog-friendly. But my dogs are rescues. They've come from difficult backgrounds, been in dogs' homes and refuges. Fleur was in a shelter twice by the age of eighteen months and Rosie had known little but being chained up and presumably being kicked, from the way she flinched every time I moved a foot too quickly when she first arrived.

Anyway, what's spoiled about having freshly, lovingly prepared fruit and vegetable smoothies for your breakfast every day if you're a dog? My dogs are on the BARF diet, which stands for Bones and Raw Food. They eat raw chicken carcasses, raw fruit and veg, eggs, cheese, yoghurt and occasionally some boiled rice for bulk. It's not practical for travelling, so on occasion they have to have dried commercial food, at which they usually turn up their noses.

And they both sleep on my bed, always. They like it. I like it. If anyone else doesn't like it or approve of it, that's fine. They don't have to sleep with us. The prospect of going away and leaving them in a kennel overnight was not one I would feel comfortable with.

A live-in pet sitter is always the ideal option. I've used the absolutely brilliant Animal Aunts in UK when I lived there, but to pay for one of them to come to France would be prohibitive. I have, of course, my great friends in the Auvergne, Tom and Chrissie, who came and babysat the cats when the dogs and I went away for a few days at a time, and they are wonderful.

Unfortunately, Rosie is wary of men and doesn't come into contact with all that many of them. When I first had her, it took me a lot of time, patience and persuasion to get her to come into the house from the garden for me, the person who fed her and let her sleep on the bed. I would worry that with a strange man in the house, she would lack the courage to do so and would have to spend a few miserable days sleeping in the garden.

Rosie was slowly coming to understand that not all people were out to hurt her, but there was one aspect of these strange human animals she had yet to come to terms with. How could they manage to change colour so often?

There seems to be some debate as to the degree of colour dogs are capable of seeing. But I can tell you that Rosie can be quite happy in the presence of a visitor like Alex or Jill, trusting enough enough to take a titbit from their hands. But let them dare to disappear upstairs then come down again with a different coloured top on. Then she has to install herself at the foot of the stairs and woof at them in great suspicion, convinced they have somehow become a different person altogether.

Fleur presents problems of her own. She loves everyone, unreservedly, and has never met a person she is remotely afraid of. The trouble with her is that she looks like a little angel but is, in fact, what the Irish call a little fecker – she runs off. Boy, does she run off! She moves with the speed of light and can be half a mile away before you realise she is no longer by your side.

Professional animal sitters, like Animal Aunts, follow an owner's instructions to the letter. But there is always the worry, with people I don't know, that because Fleur appears to be such a paragon of virtue, so well behaved when she chooses, that they might be tempted to think I was just a neurotic owner and ignore the 'keep her on the lead at all times on walks' rule.

In fact, it was another of Fleur's annoying little habits which meant that the planned trip to Italy could not, after all, take place. Fleur has always been a vocal traveller. She gets excited by going anywhere in the van. It is excitement, too, not fear. I was already convinced of that, but I got our good friend and trainer/behaviourist to come and check for me and she agreed. The barking is not Fleur-speak for 'stop the world, I want to get off'. It means, 'Oh wow, where are we going? Will it be fun? Are there things to chase? Are we going for walkies?' and so on. Not to mention the inevitable, 'Are we nearly there yet?'

Fleur's just like a small child in that she winds herself up into such a frenzy of squeaking and barking that she is utterly incapable of stopping. Within the confines of a small Renault Kangoo van, it is quite literally ear-splitting. Not so bad for Alex, who is deaf so can simply remove his hearing aids. But my hearing is one of the faculties which has not yet deserted me, and the pitch at which she barks is excruciatingly painful for me.

I have tried absolutely everything, up to and including wearing heavy duty ear defenders so I can just ignore her. Sadly, changes to French motoring laws mean that is no longer legal. After much debate, Alex and I decided we could tolerate her, just about, to go to the Vercors, but that any further would be intolerable, especially on the journey back, which we would probably make without a break. Italy would just have to go on hold until there was a Plan B.

So we loaded up the little yellow van and set off for our adventure in the wild and spectacular scenery of the Vercors. It looked as if it would have everything we needed for a perfect visit to suit us both. Military history sites for Alex? Check. Walks and wildlife for me? Check. Wolves? Check, amidst squeaks of excitement and anticipation from me, in case we were lucky enough to hear any.

We used our maps and Via Michelin online to pick what looked to be the quickest and easiest route down to the gîte I had booked for us, centrally placed for the various places we wanted to visit. We favoured motorways as much as possible for faster driving times and less twisty-turny routes for the dogs.

As we neared our destination, we could see the dramatic rugged cliff formations of a huge lump of rock springing up from the surrounding flat land. No wonder it had been such a strategically important Maquis stronghold. It commanded an impressive view for miles around.

Our journey was going well and we appeared to be within about half an hour of our destination, both looking forward to arriving in time for afternoon tea and a leg-stretch for us all. Then we came across that word which strikes fear into the hearts of motorists in France – *déviation*. Diversion. Our route should have taken us through a tunnel underneath the rocky outcrop. Unfortunately, due to rock falls, it was closed for repairs.

This meant taking to narrow, sinuous roads with plunging drops to the side of us.

'Wow! It looks really spectacular down there!'

'I am driving with my eyes firmly closed and I do not want

to know.'

But we made it, safely, though later than we had anticipated, and found our camp-site without too much difficulty. Our accommodation was part of a house, on the ground floor, and there was no one else currently in the other parts, which made it nice and quiet for us.

It was, as ever, clean and well equipped, a comfortable bedroom each, a separate loo and shower, generous kitchen area and a nice sitting area with a television. The man on reception gave me the code to access the wifi so we both sat down to check in and update our Facebook pages – only to discover there was no signal in our building for either the wifi or Alex's mobile phone.

To use it, we had to trot up the track to a little Wendy house construction with a squashy fake leather settee, the sort you sank comfortably into then needed a block and tackle to get out of. The small building was as hot as Hades, even with the door open, so our online time was going to be limited.

Our main point of interest in the Vercors was the small town of Vassieux-en-Vercors, scene of another atrocity during the war, when seventy-two inhabitants were killed in reprisals against the Maquis. It now has a Resistance Memorial, a real eyrie, high up above the cemetery where the bodies of the villagers were laid to rest. It was as moving and impressive as ever, made even more so by the dramatic and daunting terrain those young Maquisards were protecting with their lives.

We also wanted to visit the town's prehistoric museum, which houses a flint-knapping workshop, dating back nearly five thousand years. It was a fascinating visit, which illustrated so perfectly once more the much more relaxed attitude to health and safety here in France than in the UK.

Part of the visit was a live exhibition of flint-knapping, the dressing of pieces of flint into tools and weapons, using a stone hammer. We were there at the same time as a party of quite young schoolchildren. We couldn't help but be astonished at how lucky they were to see something like it, without endless safety measures in place to 'protect' them, but which would also have toned down what was such a valuable experience for them.

For a start they were sitting on real cowhide mats on the floor. I was mentally risk assessing those for possible allergies. Then they were incredibly close to the man who was working the flint, with razor sharp chips flying about close to their young, eager, upturned faces, without safety goggles, face shields or anything else.

At the point where he showed them how to make fire by striking flints into dried bulrushes in his bare hands, I gave up trying to do l risk assessments. It was simply off the Richter scale, even though he added a cursory 'don't try this at home' warning.

The children were utterly spellbound, hanging on to his every word. Inevitably, there were those who kept trying to creep even closer to the action. There were three or four teachers with the group, sitting on a row of chairs against the back wall of the room. One or other of them would simply stand up, grab the offending child by an arm, a leg or sometimes both, and haul them back to where they should be sitting.

I doubt any British teacher would dare to do the same these days. There would doubtless be screams of assault and abuse. The children didn't seem to mind in the least. There certainly no immediate sign of any of them having been maimed for life, mentally or physically.

We enjoyed our visit to the Vercors. We loved the unexpected bonus of the high cliffs opposite our windows glowing the most spectacular salmon pink, as day slipped away to evening with exquisite sunsets.

The tunnel was still closed for our return journey, so once again we were diverted up and down some incredible mountain roads, where we encountered falling snow, even in June. Alex's camera only stopped clicking for the by now familiar exchange.

'That really is a fantastic view down there.'

'I can't see any view with my eyes shut and that's fine by me, thank you very much.'

One day, we'll make it to Italy, either separately or together. It's rumoured that Doris Bird is already building the barricades.

Chapter Eighteen
Wind Beneath My Wings

As you may well remember, ear-worms are one of my, doubtless many, annoying habits. I'll hear or read a word or phrase which will instantly trigger a song in my head which will be stuck with me for hours, sometimes days. It may well be inflicted on anyone unlucky enough to be around me at the time, or even those poor souls on Facebook with whom I choose to share it.

It's genuinely beyond my conscious control. I'm sometimes blissfully unaware of doing it. I just can't help it. You only have to look at the titles of my new crime series to understand more. 'Baby's Got Blue Eyes', 'Two Little Boys', and 'When I'm Old and Grey'. You see? You're singing them now, too, aren't you?

At the time of writing this, I have the title for my fourth crime book rattling round in my head and rudely interrupting my thoughts. It's a country song, so it's lucky that I quite like them, in small doses, and fits well with the plot I have in mind. Also by chance, the singer is an ideal match for what I write about. Sometimes word association has its uses.

So you'll already have some idea of what this chapter could be about. Perhaps friendship? Illness? Heroism? It's actually more mundane than that. It's about flying. And since you should know well enough by now how much I hate it, you will know it won't be me doing the flying! Bad enough driving up mountains with my eyes closed.

My two closest friends, Alex and Jill, both love it. Alex is a former glider pilot and Jill's father was a pilot, bombers during the war and commercial aircraft after it, so she's flown all over the world. Her latest idea this year is to go wing-walking on some ancient old bi-plane. Like you do. I don't think I could even watch, but I might hold her coat.

My next-door neighbour here at the grottage is friendly and inquisitive. We sometimes don't see one another for days as our houses are back to back, so it's only if I'm in my driveway that I see her, but we always stop and chat whenever we meet.

She is also kind-hearted and animal-loving. When I lost Ci, she noticed me setting off to the vet at five in the morning, so came and rang the bell on my gate later in the day to find out what was wrong. It's reassuring to have someone like that. She is never intrusive but at least I know that if there was no sign of life here, she would notice and do something to investigate.

She always takes an interest in visits from Alex, whom she calls *Père Noël* (Father Christmas) because of his smiley face and bushy beard. We were chatting one day when I mentioned how much Alex loves flying and that he used to fly gliders in the past. She said she had a friend who was president of an *Aéroclub* in nearby Ambert, and gave me his telephone number.

I phoned him and discovered he personally runs things called *'baptêmes de l'air'*, an initiation into flying. Alex was already initiated, but they sounded ideal, as this pilot spoke some English. He said he would be happy to take Alex for a half-hour joy ride over the top of the grottage and surrounding area, so he could take photos. Right up his street, though a million miles from my idea of a fun half-hour, so I booked it.

I took Alex down to the airfield, the dogs in the back of the van, so I could take them for a walk while he did his little jolly. He told me the plane had room for three passengers so I could join them, if I wanted to. Shows how well he knows me after thirty-odd years. But he was only teasing.

I went with the chaps while they got the plane out of the hangar, a little Piper Cherokee which looked to me to be about the size of my Renault Kangoo van, with a couple of wings stuck on it. I couldn't begin to imagine how it could even get off the ground with two big burly men in it, but then I have never pretended to understand anything about how planes can fly. I prefer not even to think about it.

Trusty camera in hand, I took up position to get some pictures of the boys setting off and, hopefully, the little plane making it into the air and over the first of the mountains which lay in its path. Of course, being the Auvergne, there was absolutely no type of security visible around the place. I could, and did, wander all about the airfield and could even have ventured on to the runway, had I wanted to.

I quickly learnt to keep a watchful eye out for the tiny microlights from the next door club which used the same runway. Those little beasts, not much bigger than a European hornet, could sneak up silently behind you before you knew it.

Being superstitious, I was a bit worried when, after the pre-flight check, the little Cherokee simply coughed, spluttered and burped in response to the first turn of the key, or whatever it is you do to start an aircraft. But after a hiccup or two, it finally fired up and waddled off somewhat clumsily along the taxi-way to the runway.

Camera at the ready, I panned optimistically as it came rolling down the runway, seeming, to my untrained eye, to be going far too slowly to get off the ground, never mind over the mountain. But amazingly, it did manage to lurch into the air, where it suddenly seemed a lot perkier.

I took the dogs for a walk round the perimeter of the airfield, carefully avoiding a rather aggressive looking little aircraft from next door which I dubbed the Purple Peril. Then I put the dogs safely back in the van and took up my position to photograph the landing, which seemed to be a good, smooth one.

Soon they were rolling back along the taxi-way and I could see that the grin on Alex's face could not possibly have been any wider unless he was suffering from lockjaw. It was he, he proudly told me, who had brought the little bird down, having been entrusted to do so as he already had a few air miles under his belt from having flown one in the past.

I could see straight away that he was completely hooked. He always loved his visits to the Auvergne but now it was going to be a question as to what was the biggest draw – coming to see me, the dogs, the scenery, or going flying with his new pal.

It was great that he had found something he loved so much. On each visit now, he carefully balanced his budget to include at least one flight with Jean-Pierre, who would always take him in a different direction so he could see more and more of the region. Of course, the day they went off to fly over the volcanic chain, Alex was so excited he managed to leave not just his camera but also his smart-phone in the van, so there were no photos on that occasion.

The flights usually took place at the weekend and of course were dependent on decent weather, but we planned the rest of our outings around them easily enough. It gave us chance to explore a bit more in and around Ambert, and to discover some more nice trips, and good places to eat.

Eating out is not always easy with Silly Coeliac, and I'm constantly surprised at the times I encounter people in restaurants and selling foodstuffs who have no idea what gluten actually is. But the big advantage of the people round here is that they, mostly, genuinely want to help. And they especially want you to enjoy your food, since eating is so much a part of the way of life.

A few words with the waiting staff, sometimes a flash of my red card which sets out what I can and can't safely eat, is usually all it takes to produce a delicious meal which I can enjoy. Sometimes the chef in person will trot out of the kitchen just for clarification, which is reassuring.

After one of Alex's flying adventures, we took a run out to a part of the Livrados-Forez we had not yet explored, and on our way found a wonderful little restaurant. We made short work of a delicious meal at a reasonable price, the sort which can still be found easily enough around here. Alex is always disappointed that he can't find food, or prices, to compare when he goes back to Birmingham.

He was excited when he thought he had found a decent French restaurant, but the cost of a meal there was close to ninety pounds and the menu looked incredibly twee to me. At our favourite eatery here, *Les Chênes* (The Oaks), at Augerolles, we can enjoy a sumptuous five-course meal for less than twenty-five pounds each.

They know me well there now and I know I am always in safe hands. It's become a standing joke with Madame, who is front of house, telling me 'You can't eat that, we don't want you dying in the restaurant,' and her husband, the chef, coming out at the end of the meal and saying, 'You're still alive, then?'

It was nice to find other places where we could have lunch, especially near to the Aéroclub. But *Les Chênes* remains by far and away our favourite.

Now I knew who the pilot of the Piper Cherokee was, I started to spot the little white plane, with its blue and gold stripes, buzzing about more and more often. It must always have done so, I just hadn't noticed it before. One day it flew directly over the grottage while I was in the garden with the dogs and there was a definite waggle of the wings in greeting.

Of course, it was Murphy's Law which meant that it overflew me one day as I was walking up from the Col du Béal to Pierre sur Haute. It was chilly, I was dying to spend a penny, but I was above the tree-line so there was no cover. There were no other walkers anywhere around, so I simply moved away from the route I was following to bob down in the middle of a wide-open space.

The land up there is protected because of the diversity of the flora and fauna. There are all sorts of signs prohibiting wild camping and littering, amongst other things. I puzzled for ages over one sign. They're international symbols, often with a picture and no words, and I couldn't for the life of me imagine why there would be a sign prohibiting vomiting. The first time I saw it I couldn't get close to it as there were still snow drifts about. It took me longer than it should have done to realise what the symbol actually meant – do not pick wild flowers. The person in the drawing was actually doing exactly that, not bent double being sick, as I had imagined.

There was literally not a soul about as far as the eye could see as I got ready to relieve myself, since there were no signs prohibiting that. Until the precise moment when I dropped my draws. Then the Piper Cherokee appeared over the ridge, flying uncomfortably low and close. I've no idea how much you can see of the ground from that little plane. I will be able to tell for sure if Jean-Pierre has difficulty looking at me without going red the next time we meet.

Chapter Nineteen
Friends Old and New

I know you're all keen to find out what's been happening to some of the characters you've met in the previous *Sell the Pig* books. Particularly Kevin the Kitchen Range.

We continued our love/hate relationship through another winter. He alternately gobbled up precious firewood by burning too fast whenever it was warm, or threatened me with hypothermia by refusing to go at all when the weather was at its coldest. Not to mention his chain-smoking habit. I was going through smoke detector batteries at an alarming rate as he was forever setting them off.

Clearly, I could not continue to put up with his teenage tantrums. Kevin would have to go. The trouble was, kitchen ranges are not cheap and I was pretty much on the breadline. The disastrous investment in photovoltaic panels had left me with a whopping bank loan which the small amount they were generating was going nowhere near to covering, so I was light on funds.

Not that solar power in general is a disastrous investment. I just managed to get hooked by a rogue company who promptly went bust, having provided an inferior product which never could produce anything like as much electricity as they said it would. Certainly not enough to cover the bank loan. I still have an ongoing court case to see if I can somehow get out of the nightmare, but the other side keep asking for adjournments and

I'm no further forward now than when I started legal proceedings months ago.

Then my brother unexpectedly and generously offered to give me a contribution to buying a decent replacement range. As he rightly pointed out, it would be a false economy to invest in a cheap one which would probably turn out to be a Kevin Mark II, if not worse.

Jilli in Italy was pleased with her range, an Italian make. I liked their prices, so looked into their availability in this country. There was one company who sold them, with free delivery throughout France. But the reviews on their site were discouraging. A lot of people complained of waiting months for theirs to arrive. I didn't want any more complications in my life.

My brother offered to go with me to a supplier of different brands of ranges, which he had visited, on the far side of Clermont-Ferrand. We agreed to meet on the edge of the big city so he could pilot me in. I always turn into a complete muppet these days when driving in town. It has become something of a phobia.

I managed to demonstrate it yet again. My brother was waiting at the side of the road to show me where to park. I tried to follow his gesticulations but ended up first trying to go the wrong way up a dual carriageway, then driving along a pedestrian and cycle lane. I was lucky in that no policemen seemed to be about. It's hard to get away with much when driving a bright yellow van covered in stickers of red poppies and dragons, with slogans such as 'Where have all the hippies gone?' in the gaps.

We met close to a shopping mall and my brother suggested we have a coffee first, as the morning was cold. I'd not long had Rosie, who was still at the stage of howling forlornly every time I went out of her sight. For the first few weeks, she would even do it when I went to the loo at home. So I didn't want to leave her in the van on the car park out of my sight.

There was a KFC close by, with parking right outside the windows, so we decided to go there for a coffee. By this time, I was also quite keen to find a loo. When we got to the door, though, we discovered it was not yet open for business.

As we were peering disappointedly inside, the young manager came to the door to ask what we wanted. When we explained we were in need of hot coffee but not food, he kindly opened up and served us himself.

Going to the loo was a bit like a military assault course, as the cleaning crew were still working. Even with customers on the premises, local businesses don't often bother with warning signs or any of that 'Elf and Safety nonsense. When we were not expected, it was pretty hazardous, but even I managed not to trip over trailing cables and hoses of vacuum cleaners.

My brother had previously been to the supplier where we were heading in convoy, and spoke highly of the Austrian ranges they sold, the Lohberger brand. I'd looked them up online and they looked impressive, though expensive. Godin has traditionally been 'the' kitchen range of choice in France, but I had been told they are now made in China, although I don't know if that's true, so I was a bit dubious about them.

We had a look round the saleroom and there, in the corner, was a very stylish small Lohberger, alight and giving off a glorious glowing warmth which drew me irresistibly to it. The salesman came and chatted to us, opening and closing the doors, demonstrating the impressive Austrian engineering. The range was in a shade of metallic anthracite and managed to straddle the boundaries between solidly traditional and cutting edge modern sleek. I was hooked.

The shop could deliver and install, plus carry out all the necessarily modifications to the chimney. I signed all the papers and paid the deposit. Within a couple of weeks, two very nice young men, wearing weight-lifters' belts, came to the grottage and somehow between them managed to carry in the formidable Leo the Lohberger. Best of all, they took away

Kevin the Kitchen Range, who has now gone to smoke chimneys in the sky for evermore.

I remain somewhat in awe of Leo the Lohberger. I think he senses it and takes advantage. He is an absolute dream to light, after Kevin. Because of the swanky air wash system, he's not allowed paper, ever, in case it gets stuck in his pipes. I just put in a couple of logs, add a fire-lighter, with some kindling on top – I always use the top-down starting method for fires, which is brilliant. One match, and away he goes.

Within an hour the whole house is warm and I can start to cook on the hotplate, with the oven coming up to temperature not long behind. Such a difference from Kevin! The only slight problem so far is that I can't always manage to get him to stay in overnight. The firebox is small and the burn so efficient that it's not always possible. But the range holds the stored heat so well that it's never icy cold in the kitchen, even when Leo has gone out.

So what about your other old friends? Well, the Bowing Farmer still passes almost daily and still bows. We had a heatwave this summer, with temperatures pushing up to the forties Celsius, and I'm sure his shorts were even shorter than usual.

He looks a little disappointed as he passes these days as I've raised the height of the sight-screen along the edge of the garden, shielding me somewhat from the eyes of passing motorists. Bowing Farmer can just see me at one point as he passes on his tractor, with its higher seat.

In the four years I've now been living here, I've noticed a subtle, but important difference in the nods of greeting I get as I go about my business. Most, like the Bowing Farmer, do a chin-down nod, almost like a gesture of agreement. Others, still wary of the exotic 'foreigner' living in their midst, do a far more guarded upward motion, a chin-lift, which clearly means, 'I know who you are, but I don't know you, so I'm reserving judgement.'

The Library Ladies are still there and still delightful. They'll helpfully track down and order books for me, which is a free service here still, unlike in many parts of the UK now, I hear. They're also currently being a huge and enthusiastic help with the translation of the *Sell the Pig* series.

After the disasters of Mrs Vagina, I've found a new translator who seems to know what she's doing. Just to make sure, and to check that what she produces makes sense to a French person who has not read the original version in English, a team of Library Ladies is acting as my beta readers. They're being helped by some of my former English students, all anxious to learn all about me. Hopefully that way, we will, between all of us, produce a book in French with which to answer the question I am constantly being asked: 'Why did you leave England to move to the Auvergne?'

The French generally tend to say England rather than Britain, often meaning the whole of the British Isles. I recently read a French article about sheepdogs and how those in Wales were amongst some of the most highly-prized. Apparently, Wales is a region in the south west of England, news which will doubtless please my friends in Wales.

I'm still an active member of the local library and have now, finally, summoned up the courage to make the journey there and back on Tomato, my electric bike. Tomato has covered many, many miles, unfortunately not all of them with me on board. An intermittent fault meant the electrical assistance was prone to cutting out without warning. He was sent off to Paris twice to have it put right, although it made no difference.

On an electric Sole bike, you still have to pedal all the time to get the assistance. Unless you are whizzing down the steep hill into Olliergues, when it is actually impossible to pedal fast enough to keep up with the rate at which the wheels go round. The big disadvantage of the bike is that, if it breaks down and you have to pedal home, it's very heavy. It's only five kilometres each way but there's a lot of uphill.

I always have to remind myself of Tomato's other little peculiarity, before I set off down the big, steep hill. He can be collapsed and folded in half for travelling in a vehicle. I generally remember to check most things before I set off, like the tyre pressures and the brakes. But I often forget to check the wing nut which holds the handlebars upright or enables them to be folded down for travelling.

It takes me far too long these days, as I wobble on my way, thinking the steering doesn't feel quite as responsive and positive as it should, to realise that the wing nut has come loose. Too much pressure on the hand grips and I could find the handlebars folding over as I speed on my merry way down the big hill. I think the answer might be to make and laminate a sign to myself to hang on to the basket at the front.

'Tighten wing nut, you nut!'

Lately, though, perhaps now Kevin is no longer here to egg him on to bad behaviour, Tomato has been utterly angelic and I'm even able to come flying back up the big hill in top gear all the way.

Whenever I go to the library, I always head straight for the crime section, my favourite to read as well as to write. I always read in French and have become paranoid about translations, having encountered some really bad examples in what I have read, not to mention my own disasters in that area.

I like Ian Rankin's books, especially the Rebus series, although I find the Rebus character hard to like as a person. I still wonder how he's kept his driving licence, let alone his job, with the amount he drinks, even when driving. In one of the books, Rebus says something like, 'I don't think we're in Kansas any more,' to which faithful sidekick Siobhan replies, 'Does that make me Toto?'

The translator clearly didn't bother to check his facts, as his footnote goes into details about Toto, the American rock band of the 1970s. Surely everyone knows that if the words Kansas and Toto appear in the same sentence, Toto has to be a reference to the dog in The Wizard of Oz?

I'm determined to avoid any such gaffes in my translations, so the Library Ladies and my former students are on hand to go through the drafts and spot any suggestion of a slip-up or misunderstanding. I'm sure there won't be any. I have every faith in my new translator. I checked before signing the contract that she knew her dogs from her rock bands.

And on the subject of old friends, those of you who follow me on Facebook often ask, 'Who is Robin and do you two really hate one another? And where do the pigs come into it?' That's because our frequent exchanges there might seem, to those not in the loop, as if we are deadly enemies.

Many moons ago, when young Robin was nobbut a lad and I was a grown-up teenager who taught at the local riding school, I had the privilege, if you can call it that, of giving him his first-ever lesson. It was on a pony called Rajah, I seem to remember.

When he got a bit bigger, he also joined the staff at the stables. There were other boys who helped out, too, but for some reason, Robin was always the one us girls liked to pick on.

The stables were at Halliday Hill Farm, in Offerton, an important building as it was the home of the Dodge family who went on to found Dodge City in the USA. It was built on a hill, so the land sloped steeply away from the outbuildings. We hung out in the tack room, mostly, which was situated about six feet up above a small paddock where the pigs were turned out.

I remember three pigs, Lucinda, a docile Large White, and two spotty ones, Spot and Engel. Engel had a particularly nasty temper. Our favourite trick, or perhaps it was a scientific experiment, was to see if one annoying teenage boy could run faster than a very grumpy Gloucester Old Spot boar when we repeatedly tossed Robin unceremoniously down the six-foot drop into the pig pen.

He always did survive, which is how he now comes to be following me on Facebook, where I refer to him equally as Pig Boy or Stupid Boy. They are, after a fashion, terms of endearment.

And yes, if you've seen mention of it on Facebook, I really did once break his knee playing a particularly vicious game of Split the Kipper. I make no apology. But you may have noticed that I've dedicated this book to him as a token recompense.

Chapter Twenty
Égalité

Equality is something I'm passionate about. For everything. After all, I chose to become French and it is part of our national motto, *Liberté, Égalité, Fraternité*. Liberty, Equality, Fraternity. I don't think anyone should be prevented from doing or saying what they want because of their gender, sexuality, race, age, disability or anything else.

As I've said before, disabled access is still in its infancy here, especially in the more rural areas. But we've generally found that it's been cancelled out by the naturally kind and helpful nature of the people we encounter. I do tend to go off the deep end sometimes, though, when it ought to be better than it is.

One place I wanted to take Alex to was the Gour de Tazenat, the volcanic lake not far from the Pink House. It was always a favourite place of mine for wild camping. Ci and I would cosy down in the back of the van, high above the lake, and watch the moon and stars through the back window. On one occasion the enthusiastic scratching of a wild boar against the van nearly sent us plunging down the slope into the water.

I've never been back to the Pink House since I moved out. I still meet my brother periodically for coffee or a meal. But that house holds more bad memories than good for me, so I prefer to leave it in the past. Not to mention the fact that he has never been any good at housework and he now has a dozen or more semi-feral cats living there with him, so it is probably best avoided.

Alex and I took a slightly roundabout route to get to the lake when we visited, in order to avoid driving past the Pink House. The lake is near the small village of Charbonnières-les-Vieilles, the one an online translator had memorably rendered as Coal Scuttle the Old Ladies.

It's never a good idea to rely on any form of automated translator for anything. I was recently Facebook chatting to a friend who I know is learning French. I signed off as I would to a French friend here, with something colloquially affectionate which would be the equivalent in English of 'Laters, chucky hen.'

I was rendered helpless and very nearly incontinent by her puzzled response which asked why I was saying, 'More my casseroles.'

Once we passed there, I confidently swung the van up the hill to the narrow tarmac road which would take up us to the high vantage point above the lake.

Only the road wasn't there. There were big boulders across where I thought the access point had been and there appeared to be no sign of tarmac, only trees and grass. It was only just over three years since I had last been there. Surely a road could not have completely disappeared in that time?

But it seemed it had. Presumably in an attempt to protect the fragile landscape, the road had been closed off and allowed to revert to nature. It was amazing to see how quickly undergrowth had sprung up everywhere, so the road was already little more than a memory.

As ever, I had a Plan B. I usually have up to about Plan Q in my head for any outing. I knew from taking my mother there that disabled access to the lakeside was not easy. Mother weighed about seven stone wringing wet and I had even found it tough pushing her in the wheelchair along the stony access tracks. Seventeen stone of Alex might be too much, even for my enthusiasm.

I turned the van round, retraced our steps, and set off to find another small track on the other side of the lake. It would bring us to the highest point above the lake with the best views, the exact spot where Ci and I had camped so many times. I was hoping that it would still be there and accessible.

The track was there all right, but as I drove slowly down it, I could see ahead of us a wooden barrier, completely blocking the lane. Everywhere was overgrown since I'd last been there, so there was no way round it on either side and it was exactly the wrong height to get a wheelchair under. Thwarted!

We'd come all this way, so we were not about to depart without at least a glimpse of the lake. Another U-turn, then off back down the hill, to park at the side of the road and prepare to tackle the rocky road with the wheelchair.

Alex walked where he could, I shoved where he couldn't, and we did manage to get to the water's edge. But the best views of the lake are from high above. It's a volcanic maar, or lake, eighty metres deep, with sixty-six metres of water depth, and a diameter of seven hundred metres. The view from above, with the volcanic chain in the background, is stunning. But even had the road up still been there, its gradient was impossible for a wheelchair.

Although he was clicking away merrily with his camera, I could see that Alex was disappointed not to have had the best of the views. Time for one last try. We drove back round to the track with the barrier and I left the van in one of the disabled parking spaces, a new feature there, which should have given me a clue.

Rule No 1, Tottie, you silly tart – never take anything at face value. When I walked along the track, I found that what had looked, from a distance, to be a single, solid barrier, was in fact two staggered poles, with a gap between them which would just about allow a wheelchair through. Alex got his spectacular view of the lake from up above, and we enjoyed a picnic there.

We sat on a big wooden structure which was an engraving with details about the region. With the disabled parking spaces and access, it was a particularly bizarre bit of planning, since it was impossible for a wheelchair user to see the detail on the tableau, unless they were able to get out of their chair and stand, as Alex was.

One place where there is no excuse for poor disabled access is a big modern supermarket. I've had problems before with one of the large chain-stores in Thiers, and I'm not the only one. Unhelpful, unfriendly staff who clearly don't understand that without customers, they would have no jobs. One experience there with Alex led to me going for a meeting with the store director and him putting a rocket up several backsides with, I'm pleased to say, some positive results.

I don't like shopping in the big supermarkets. I'm a confirmed locavore and supporter of small, independent shops. Unfortunately, Silly Coeliac greatly restricts where I can do my shopping. Take chocolate for example. Yes, please! I love chocolate, I eat some daily. But so many brands contain traces of gluten, so I can't have them. My local shop has none at all which I can safely eat, and of the shelves and shelves of it in the local supermarket I visit, there is only one brand which is safe for me, and not all of the ones it makes are gluten free. Hence the need to visit the bigger stores.

On this occasion, I needed some cider to make a chicken dish Alex is particularly fond of. He was, as ever, in the wheelchair so he could get round the big store easily. We were in the drinks aisles and I headed to where the overhead sign announced '*Cidre*.' No cider. Only beer. Nothing remotely apple-based to be found.

We split up and started up and down the various aisles which may logically contain cider, starting with where the lighter beers like lager and the shandies were stacked. Still no cider. More in hope than anticipation, I went in search of a member of staff, as I have never found them to be either approachable or helpful in that store.

True to form, the assistant I found merely asked if I had looked on the 'Cider' shelves. Yes, I explained, that was, naturally, the first place I had looked. With an audible sigh and a tut, she strutted off in that direction, without a word to me, so I merely followed behind. I enjoyed the look on her face when she discovered for herself that despite the overhead sign, there was no cider on the '*Cidre*' shelf.

Eventually, she tracked the cider down to the champagne shelf. Of course, silly me, if I wanted cheap cider to cook a chicken in, I should have known it would be among the pricey bottles of champagne. Still with barely a word to me, certainly not a, 'Sorry for the inconvenience, it wasn't where it should be,' the woman stalked off back to the front of the store.

I went to find Alex and we headed for the checkouts, as we'd now found everything we had come for. As usual, there were queues at all of them and although we went and stood plaintively by the specially adapted disabled access checkout, no one appeared to open it for us. In fact the same woman as earlier, Miss Congeniality, waved us impatiently to another checkout, then snapped at me as we inadvertently joined the queue at the one reserved for holders of the store's own credit card. She pointed us to the next one.

The problem was, it was not disabled-friendly. So not only was it too high for Alex to pack his own shopping, it was too narrow for him to wheel himself through, and he banged both his elbows in the attempt. This actually seemed to rather amuse Miss Congeniality.

My English friend from Olliergues, Avril, had also had problems at the same store. As a result, she had been to see the director who had apologised and presented her with a bouquet of flowers and a bottle of wine. For me, it was not about compensation, not even about an apology. It was about putting things right. *Égalité*, after all, should mean that a wheelchair user could do their own shopping without things being made unnecessarily difficult for them. I fired off a fairly blistering email to the director, not really anticipating any great success, but just needed to vent my spleen.

I was surprised and pleased to get a fairly swift response by telephone. It was a new store director, who had not long taken over, and who invited me to go into the store and talk through my issues with him.

As soon as I saw the man striding down the corridor to greet me at the store, I could tell he wasn't a local. He was tall, wearing a fashionably tight shiny suit, expensive leather loathers, and a woollen scarf tied round his neck, even indoors. He confirmed my suspicion later when he said he was from Paris.

He sat and listened politely to my account, agreeing with me that his inherited staff left a lot to be desired in the customer relations department. He summoned his staff manager to hear what I had to say. He asked if I would mind if he pinned up my email in the staff room, in an attempt to show them how important customer feedback was. I was happy to agree.

After many apologies and a voucher for my next shopping trip there, he shook my hand and I went on my way. Things have definitely improved there. They know who I am, of course. I often encounter Miss Congeniality at the checkouts and she is always at pains to greet me with a polite, '*Bonjour, madame*,' and to add the customary '*bonne journée*', good day, when I leave. I suspect there is a wax effigy of me with pins in it in the staff room, next to my email of complaint. Or a photo of me taking the place of a dart board.

But perhaps other customers, especially wheelchair users, may be getting a better experience shopping there as a result of my actions, so it is all to the good.

Chapter Twenty-one
Times Are A-changing

Part of the big attraction of the Auvergne for me has always been its peace and tranquillity. It's a cliché, but there's no better way of saying it. It's like the Britain of fifty years ago. Well, certainly out in the sticks, as we are here.

I'd got used to going out with the dogs without ever locking the door. I frequently left the van unlocked, not always intentionally. The crime rate is low. I've lived in rural parts of the UK where break-ins and thefts of vehicles were, if not commonplace, certainly not unusual. But here in sleepy Olliergues and its outlying villages and hamlets, that aspect of the twenty-first century had not yet fully manifested itself. Until recently.

I'm not getting into a debate here, or anywhere else, about the whys and wherefores, or who is to blame. Times are getting harder for most people and desperate times lead to desperate measures, although, of course, not everyone resorts to crime to get through them.

One day my neighbour told me that there had recently been break-ins and car thefts in a nearby sleepy village. Cars, normally left unlocked, sometimes even with the keys in, had been taken for a drive round, a joy-ride, sometimes left burnt out, even newer, expensive models.

One had clearly been used for a burglary of a small supermarket, as after the break-in, the car had been found abandoned, full of sweets which had been stolen from the shop. My neighbour and I speculated over the fence dividing our properties as to who would do that and why. The consensus was that it was probably younger people from the bigger towns. I suggested they may have been stoned and smitten with the munchies.

All this happened just after I'd had five *steres* (cubic metres) of firewood delivered and dumped in my driveway for me to barrow to the barn. That's quite a lot of firewood and quite hard going, shoving it down there by the barrow-load. I had been in no hurry to do it, planning to take my time and to leave the van parked on the verge outside until I was finished.

The news changed all that. My little van might not be all that exciting but it was a sitting target out on the road. I decided to shift as much wood as it took so that I could get little Roo the Kangoo safely back inside the gate. I measured carefully the width of the van, trying to allow for the already difficult angle for backing in, to know how much of the wood-stack I would need to move before I could get the van off the road.

I was both pleased and proud when I managed to clear just sufficient of the logs, and to do the tight manoeuvre, so that I could back in and still manage to close the gates. Of course, silly tart that I am, I completely forgot to allow for opening the van door to get out. I couldn't even crawl out of the sliding side door as Fleur's travel cage, bought at vast expense in the vain hope of her travelling more quietly in it, was in the way. So I had to do some extremely ungainly wriggling over the seats and the cage to get out of the back door. And that involved getting slightly more intimately acquainted with both gear lever and hand brake than I would have chosen.

It wasn't just the joyriders disturbing the peace and security, either. Friends of mine had quite a fright recently. They run a B&B not far from here, a lovely house on several storeys, with entrance doors in several places. Madame had gone out shopping, leaving Monsieur, who is hard of hearing, home alone.

On her return, she found two young people, a man and a woman, in her front garden, armed with leaflets about jewellery. They claimed to be selling it on behalf of a large supermarket chain. They were not French, their command of the language was not brilliant, and the story was clearly a load of hogwash.

With great presence of mind, Madame locked the car quickly, with her handbag inside it. The young woman was insistently trying to get her to fill in a form to order some jewellery, and equally insistent that she should open the car to get out a pen with which to do so.

By now, a third person, another young man, had appeared and was wandering off up some of the steps towards another side entrance into the house.

Fortunately, my friends are ex-teachers who have travelled abroad extensively to teach. It was going to take more than three not-much-older-than-teenagers to intimidate Madame. She sent them firmly on their way then phoned the police, who came round to take details.

Yes, there's another difference to how things are here, still, compared to how I found it when last I lived in the UK. Because here, the gendarmes do come round, often very speedily, in response to your call, sometimes even when no crime has been committed, only an attempt at one.

It was clearly no coincidence that the same night, three shops on the main street in Olliergues were broken into. We hadn't had anything like it in our sleepy little town before, certainly not in the four years since I had bought my grottage. The nearest thing was a near-neighbour who had a lawnmower and a brush-cutter pinched from an unlocked outbuilding. Because of it, I now lock my door and shut the windows when I go out, even just for a short walk with the dogs. A sad sign of the times.

Of all the trappings of modernity I least expected to arrive in Le Mas, after fibre optic, it was this tiny little *lieu-dit* finding itself as the host venue for a rave. A *lieu-dit* is the French version of one of those little settlements that are barely large enough to be a hamlet. The sort where you can't quite imagine why they sprang up where they did.

We have a small pond in Le Mas, where people come fishing and, of course, the hunters are always active round and about. There are various reasonably well way-marked footpaths here and there, and the communal bread oven is a historic feature which attracts some visitors. Other than that, not many people come to Le Mas.

There are a handful of younger, working families, but also quite a few retirees. And when the old *mamies*, grannies, come up from town for the summer months, the average age shoots up. Not exactly your typical rave venue.

It happened on the Summer Solstice weekend. The dogs and I had, as ever, gone away wild camping overnight, so we were blissfully unaware, until we arrived home early afternoon on the Sunday. As I got out of the van and let the dogs out, I could hear loud and insistent 'whoomp-whoomp' music from lower down in the hamlet. I just assumed the younger couple who lived down there had friends round for a barbecue and had their sound system turned up a bit high.

As soon as she heard my van pull up, my neighbour appeared to tell me all about it. When she said it was a rave, I did a double take, thinking I'd misunderstood her, although the French use the same word.

My neighbour has more insatiable curiosity than Kipling's Elephant's Child, so had already taken her little dog for a walk over towards where the rave was taking place. She said there was litter scattered about everywhere, drinks bottles and cans, food wrappers and the like. She also told me that as there were an estimated three hundred people there, with no proper sanitary provisions, there was other litter which was much worse. Especially as we were undergoing a real heatwave, with temperatures brushing the forties.

Young people had been turning up from the nearby city of Clermont-Ferrand and beyond, because the rave was advertised online. They'd been pitching tents anywhere the fancy took them, sometimes in people's gardens, without asking. One farmer had turned some away just as they were about to avail themselves of one of his outbuildings as a latrine.

Strangely, and slightly worryingly, the rave had apparently happened with the knowledge and consent of the *mairie*, the town hall, and there was permission to hold further raves there. We, the residents of the hamlet, had not been informed, let alone consulted.

We had recently acquired a new, young mayor, in his late twenties. Perhaps he was hoping for more votes from younger people by showing his progressive side.

My neighbour and I agreed that most of us could probably put up with the noise once or twice a year. After all, we'd all been young ourselves at one time. I'd never been into raves, or their equivalent, in my day, but I'd certainly done my share of rowdy parties and loud music. But none of us was keen on the lack of respect for the property of others. And certainly not on our nice little not-quite-a-hamlet being turned into one giant outdoor lavatory.

There hasn't been another rave in the hamlet, so far. Nor have we heard if there will be. If I get wind of it, the dogs and I will simply pack up and go off wild camping for the night in question. I'm getting too old for that sort of thing. And this noise the young things call music. Now if it was a decent bit of Queen … I'd better stop here on this subject. I'm starting to sound too much like my mother!

Something else brought Le Mas notoriety as well as the rave and that was something even less attractive. Ragweed.

Ragweed is a pernicious weed in the Ambrosia genus of the aster family, *Ambroisie* in French. It can cause serious allergic reactions in people and animals, especially acute respiratory problems. There was just a possibility that it could have been a trigger for the fatal pulmonary oedema which killed my dog, Ci, as he died in September when the ragweed pollen count is at its highest.

Because his death was sudden and unexpected, the vet had asked permission to carry out a post-mortem examination to see if she could find a cause. Other than confirming her diagnosis of pulmonary oedema, nothing was revealed by way of a definite cause, but the plant was still a prime suspect.

It turned out that Le Mas had one of the highest concentrations of the weed in the area. Television cameras headed our way and there was a piece on early evening TV to show what it looked like and to warn viewers of the dangers.

As well as respiratory problems, it can trigger severe hay fever, eczema, urticaria and conjunctivitis. Those involved in the filming were gloved and masked as if dealing with a deadly toxin. It was pretty impressive.

My neighbour, that fount of all knowledge, had what seemed to be a plausible explanation for how we suddenly had so much of it in the hamlet. The work to lay the underground fibre optic cables had involved digging up the verges in places, rather than ripping up roads, to lay them underneath. The restitution work had involved bringing in lorry loads of topsoil from elsewhere.

Was it possible that this topsoil was contaminated with ragweed seeds? Quite likely, I would imagine, with its sudden proliferation after the work was carried out.

Luckily most of it was growing lower down the hill in the hamlet and I wasn't affected. I was always careful not to walk the dogs down there during pollen time, even if that was not the cause of losing Ci.

Joining the twenty-first century high technology was no consolation for losing my little buddy.

Chapter Twenty-two
This Way Up

The iconic landmark of the Puy de Dôme region is the volcano after which it is named, the Puy de Dôme itself. Despite his many visits here, Alex had not yet reached its summit, although he had photographed it from every conceivable angle, near and far. Clearly, that needed to change.

When I was still living at the Pink House, Alex had visited with another mutual friend, Young Bobby. We'd had a snowy visit to the Massif du Sancy, then driven back via the Puy to see if it was possible to drive up it. The ice and snow made it out of the question, and it was certainly not a drive I would have wanted to attempt with my eyes firmly closed for the worst of the drops.

I've made it to the summit, twice. Once on the scary coach ride, with my brother, another time on foot with a visiting friend. We chose the slightly longer but less punishing route than simply yomping up the steep mule track, which a surprising number of hardy souls opt for. I did know a young man who was training to join the *gendarmes* by running up and down it several times a day with a full kit bag on his back. Each to their own.

I hadn't been able to get Alex up to the top yet because the council had decided to install a cog railway to the summit. All vehicular tourist traffic to the top was suspended for two years while the work was carried out.

It was an ambitious project, part of plans to get World Heritage status for the whole Chaîne des Puys volcanic chain, of which the Puy de Dôme is the highest point, coupled with the Limagne Fault plain close by. The Puy, twinned with Mount Fuji in Japan, is one of France's most visited sites, and all that road traffic was taking its toll on it, environmentally speaking.

Building the five kilometre rail track to the summit cost around eighty-six million Euros. It had a somewhat ignominious launch when one of the first trains up jumped the track at the top, which meant that the system had to shut while it was recovered and repairs were made. It was followed, not long after, by unprecedented rainfall washing out the ground under the tracks in places, with another enforced closure.

I left it long enough for it to work through all of its teething troubles before proposing that Alex and I should go and ride the beast to the summit. Because it was so new, opened in 2012, and because of the World Heritage status application, there was a good chance that facilities for the disabled would be good.

I managed to navigate my way through Clermont-Ferrand, never a certainty, and soon we were on the long and twisting road which would take us up to the new visitor centre and car park at the Puy. I could probably have driven right up to the visitor centre entrance to deposit my wheelchair-using passenger, before going to park the van. But we opted for the car park and as usual, friendly, helpful French people, seeing little me pushing big Alex, stopped and offered to help. In fact we managed fine between us, Alex wheeling and me shoving.

The visitor centre was very swish, and as we had hoped, everything was easily wheelchair accessible. We bought our train tickets then, with ten minutes or so to spare, had a look round and a quick visit to the gift shop.

When we arrived on the platform, an attendant immediately took us in charge, because of the wheelchair. We were assisted on to the train before anyone else and Alex and chair were safely parked in a designated area, while I sat in the next seat. Very impressive.

The train was wonderful, gliding along quietly and pollution free, up the ascent. The views were magnificent and I was surprised Alex didn't get Repetitive Strain Injury in his camera shutter finger, the amount of photos he took.

When we arrived at the top, we were directed towards a disabled lift which would take us up to the exterior for the views and the food outlets. Here the views had gone up a notch from magnificent to spectacular, with a three hundred and sixty degree panorama, which was positively breathtaking.

One of the walkways with the best views had a railing around it, because of the dramatic drop on the other side. It's called a *garde-fou* in French, literally a 'protect the crazy'. It had a sign on it, helpfully warning us that, during a thunderstorm, it was not a good idea to hold on to the metal rail. As my Canadian friend Heather would say, 'No shit, Sherlock.'

And speaking of crazies, there were plenty of those in evidence, jumping happily off the top with only a couple of hopefully rip-stop nylon wings to hold them up. I believe they call it hang-gliding. I prefer to call it utter insanity. They take people on rides, too. The instructors take passengers, strapped to them. Not even to enjoy such intimate contact with fit young men could I endure that form of torture.

Surprisingly, despite his love of flying, I couldn't persuade Alex to have a go, although I promised to hold his coat for him. His excuse was that he would be too heavy and with the combined weight of him and the instructor, they would never get off the ground.

We had a good look round everywhere that was accessible, but gave the ruins of the Temple of Mercury, right at the summit itself, a miss, as they were not so easy to push the wheelchair to. We paid the price of a three-course meal anywhere else for a baguette for Alex, some crisps for me and a bottle of water each, then headed back towards the platform to get the next train down.

We came up with no trouble at all, so going down should be just as easy, right? Wrong! The same care and planning had somehow not gone into the access at the summit for disabled people as down below at the visitor centre. We headed confidently back to the lift we had come up in. As it arrived at our level, Alex started to wheel himself in – and very nearly tipped over flat on his face. The lift didn't quite align properly with where we were standing. We hadn't noticed so much coming up, probably because I had semi-automatically, tipped the chair back to set the front wheels onto the platform outside.

Between us, we managed to cope, but Alex was a bit shaken up and not best pleased. The lift took us down to the level of the platform. It wasn't until we got down there and saw there was a barrier between us and the train we needed to be boarding that we realised it was an up only lift, although there was nothing at the top to tell us that.

Back to the upper level once more, and again the same poor alignment problem. It took me behind tilting the chair to get it up over the lip. It would not have been possible for Alex on his own. Then I went trotting off by myself to see if I could find the right lift to take us down. I did eventually find one which said 'To the trains' on the door, so we made it down to the platform, where the earlier train had departed and we had to wait for the next one.

We made it home, back through the city, and ticked off yet another must-see from our list. It's lucky that the Auvergne has so many natural wonders. With most of my visitors in their sixties, like me, I doubt we'll run out of places to go and things to see in our lifetime.

My best friend Jill still makes her annual visit for a week, usually in July. She is four days younger than me, which she never lets me forget, and it's nice to spend our birthdays together, usually celebrating with a good meal.

One place she and I enjoy visiting is the spa and swimming pools at Royat, on the far side of Clermont-Ferrand. It's wonderfully therapeutic to spend a couple of hours wallowing in warm, bubbling, volcanic water, or swimming in either the indoor or outdoor pool.

Jill is an excellent strong swimmer. I learnt later in life and am not very good, although I enjoy trying. The pools have mill races, bubbly bits and strong overhead showers, which create quite a strong current. I can often find myself kicking away for what seems like ten minutes just to get from one side of the pool to the other. Meanwhile Jill has probably lapped me a dozen times. But being determined, I always get there in the end.

Not all of my visitors are older. 2015 was finally the year I had a visit from my good friend and long-term copywriting colleague, Sarah. We'd known each other since the turn of the millennium when I first started doing some work for her as a freelance. She'd paid a visit to the Pink House not long after I first moved out to France. She had been promising for ages to come and see me at the grottage, and this was the year she managed it. She came with her eleven-year-old daughter, Maisie.

Rosie was just about getting used to visitors, as long as they didn't change colour too often. She'd never met anything quite as alarming as a very energetic small girl who loves gymnastics and dancing and who seemed, to Rosie, to spend as much time standing on her hands as on her feet. It was a step too far for Rosie, who could only cope with strange human beings the right way up. She spent a lot of time looking at her in bewilderment from the far side of the garden, not daring to come any closer.

On walks out, I put Maisie in charge of Fleur and she rose brilliantly to the challenge. Fleur is a difficult and determined dog to work, with a strong mind of her own. Once Maisie had got used to the idea that there's no point asking Fleur to do anything, you have to tell her, firmly and insistently, they got on like a house on fire.

We went for long walks with the dogs, all around where I live. Once the dogs were suitably tired out, I took my visitors round Olliergues to show them the quirky narrow streets, the ancient buildings, and the place where the pavers had made a stone flower outside the bar which had given them drinks while they worked.

Maisie was interested and knowledgeable. What she didn't know, she was able to make an intelligent guess at. She was curious and into everything. For someone with acrophobia (fear of heights), like me, there's only one thing worse than looking at a drop, and that's watching someone else standing on the edge of somewhere, looking at a drop.

I took them up to the ancient château which had, in its day, been the schoolhouse for the town. It sits high up on a lump of volcanic rock and commands an important strategic point. There are, of course, some impressive drops down the ramparts. Watching Maisie scamper about on the walls like a chamois turned my knees to jelly on a few occasions.

Of course, we raided the soap factory, since no visit to the area is complete without going there and inevitably coming away with about a year's supply of the exquisitely fragrant soap.

I'd been making a conscious effort to take more exercise, having turned into a total blob over the winter. A combination of writing crime fiction non-stop like a thing possessed, often being snowed in, or at least iced in, and Rosie not being brave enough to venture far in her new surroundings, had kept dog walkies to a minimum.

Determined to do my recommended ten thousand steps a day, I'd even bought myself a pedometer. Between us, my visitors and I did twice that. The weather was kind, we had all our meals in the garden, looking across at the Chaîne des Puys and the Puy de Dôme in particular, with the spectacular sunsets behind it.

I think they got it. The attraction. The reason I hope to live out the rest of my days right here.

Chapter Twenty-three
Bad Hair Day

Especially since I have retired from copywriting, I spend far more time than I ought to on social media. For a writer of books (I hate the word author, but more of that anon), it's such a great way to interact with readers who might otherwise remain anonymous.

Although I include my email address in my books so people can contact me, most contact is through social media and it's wonderful. I often get Tweets and messages from readers saying what they thought about one of my books. The ending of my second crime novel, Two Little Boys, was deliberately ambiguous, and a few people contacted me wanting to know if their interpretation was correct.

Some people go on to leave reviews, which is always much appreciated. I don't think readers realise quite how much a writer enjoys a bit of feedback. We spend weeks, months, sometimes years, sweating blood to produce our work and then sometimes, there's nothing but a deafening silence. I personally don't mind whether the feedback is good or bad. I just love to feel I've moved someone enough to make a comment of sorts.

Social media somehow seems to break down barriers, so people will chat readily with someone they might not otherwise encounter. Of course, it is also a place for seemingly vacuous so-called celebrities to post things of no possible interest to those of us who neither know nor care who they are.

Take selfies, for instance. Personally, I don't. I don't have a camera on my phone. It can make and receive calls and texts and that's its limit. And it only does that when it can find a signal, which is not all that often. A lot of my ten thousand steps per day target is taken up by scampering round the garden waving my mobile aloft, trying to get a signal.

Alex often posts photos of me when he's visiting but they usually involve one or more dogs or some particularly delicious meal we are enjoying. The talented designer of my book covers always despairs of me as I scratch round to find some sort of a mugshot to go with my mini-biography. He's very clever at getting rid of dogs' ears or delicious puddings like *ile flottant*, so the reader can concentrate on me. Though why they would want to is another of life's mysteries.

One particular manifestation of the selfies craze had me foaming at the mouth in fury, but definitely putting my money where my mouth was, so to speak.

Various 'celebs' were busy posting their selfies, showing them with no make-up on, as if this was some huge self-sacrifice on their part. Apparently it was done as part of some sort of campaign to raise awareness of breast cancer. The message was lost on me, and I suspect on many others. All I saw were vacuous people making a big issue of not yet having put on their make-up. Big deal. I never wear make-up, so I couldn't really understand what was so noble about being snapped without any.

I always said that if I were to make some sort of gesture on behalf of a charity, or an illness or some such, it would be something significant, like shaving off my hair. Little did I know what was heading my way.

As part of a general surge in highlighting breast cancer in a practical and useful way, a friend put a post on her Facebook time-line of how to self-diagnose for it. It was interesting, as it wasn't confined to looking for the lump which one assumes is the most common early warning sign. There were other indicators there, several of which I would not have thought of as being significant.

I shared the post. Another friend, Linda, read it, recognised one of the symptoms listed, and promptly took herself off to see her doctor. There was good news and bad news. The bad news was she definitely did have a more unusual form of cancer. The good news was that she was doing something about it, relatively early on.

The speed with which the formidable French healthcare service rolled into action on Linda's behalf was impressive. It seemed she barely had time to go home and pack a nightie between getting the diagnosis and going into hospital to begin the treatment. It was going to be swift and radical – surgery, then chemotherapy, then radiotherapy, then ongoing hormone therapy and re-constructive surgery, should it be required.

The oncologist sat down with Linda, in typical French pro-active fashion, to go through the list of medication to be used and the known side-effect of each type. I'd heard so many horror stories of chemo in the UK where the side-effects are so unpleasant that people have stopped the treatment. Here, it's more a case of, 'the side effect of this is usually this, but we will give you this at the same time to counteract the unpleasant symptoms'.

One side-effect, he did warn her, was unavoidable – she would lose her hair, and there was nothing he could do about it. She has two attractive daughters who both immediately offered to shave off their lovely luxuriant locks in solidarity with their mum.

Linda wouldn't hear of it and nor would I. My hair has always, once past the soft, baby-fluff stage, been as wiry as a Brillo pad on a bad hair day. And as rebellious as I am. I often wondered if it was, in no small measure, due to Mother's efforts with the scissors in our kitchen when I was a child. Mother had many talents, particularly interior design. Sadly, hairdressing was not one of them.

Whether I pay for a cheap and cheerful quick *brushing*, as the French call a cut and blow dry, or I spend a vast amount to go to some chic hair stylist, the result is always the same. A wiry, partially unravelled pan scourer, sticking out in all directions. Or Nigel Kennedy, having just stuck his finger in an electrical socket. Who knows? Shaving it off and starting again may even be a good idea.

Alex, who was staying with me at the time, was delighted, in a sadistic sort of way, to be handed the clippers and pressed into service to shave off the bits I couldn't reach.

It was summer time, so getting rid of my unruly pan-scrub was no great hardship. In fact, I quite enjoyed being without hair. I'm not sure whether it was flattering or not when Alex said it suited me so much he actually preferred me without hair!

Our first outing afterwards was fine, as it was to the annual country music festival in Courpiere. I merely wore the Stetson I had brought back from Alberta when I went on a sponsored ride in the Canadian Rockies in aid of Guide Dogs for the Blind. After that I either covered up if I was in danger of putting people off their food or went hatless, despite Alex constantly telling me I would fry my brains and get sunstroke, neither of which has ever happened.

Meanwhile Linda was busy making preparations for losing her lovely ashy-grey hair, which included going to be fitted for a wig. We met up for coffee and a catch-up soon after, as we often do, either just the two of us or with one or other of our usual coven of close friends.

I'm the sort of friend who would do anything I could to help someone, but I'm rubbish at knowing the 'appropriate' thing to say. I was constantly told at school that I had no sense of decorum and it's true, I don't. I tend to see something funny in even the darkest of circumstances, and my sense of humour is decidedly warped.

It's a good job Linda is well used to me, and that often we

meet up in places where we are the only English speakers. I'm sure some people who don't know us would have been horrified at some of the conversations which had us laughing like silly things.

Linda told us of her initial visit to a possible wig-maker she had been recommended, where she was put off by the sight of the man in the waiting room who seemed to be wearing a dead cat on his head.

Matching the exact hair colour seemed to be quite a precise art. When I heard that the wig-maker spent a lot of time on the phone to her supplier discussing Linda's lovely shade, I got an absurd attack of the giggles. I was imaging a conversation along the lines of, 'You know that Persian cat you said was a bit under the weather? Well, how's it feeling now? I've got a possible match.'

Linda came through the treatment with incredible fortitude, with never a word of complaint. The wig she finished up getting was stylish and flattering and I'm reliably informed that no cats were harmed in the making of it. Her own hair grew back quite quickly and she kept it in that timeless ultra-short style which Mia Farrow probably first made fashionable and which gets called urchin, pixie or gamine, amongst other names.

My hair? It grew back as before, as coarse and wild as steel wool rocking a Nigel Kennedy, being electrocuted by his own violin, during an electric storm.

Chapter Twenty-four
What's In a Name?

I've been known as Tottie Limejuice for years. My first-ever email account was in that name and these days, most people call me Tottie or Tots. Although my book cover designer was amused when I recently dashed off a quick email to him and he assumed, kindly, that it was auto-correct, the dreaded 'spill chucker', which had replaced the O with an I. Sadly, it was just more evidence of how senile I am getting as I approach my dotage.

I'd always claimed Tottie Limejuice was an invention of my Auntie Ethel, as she was the only person I'd ever heard use the phrase, 'She comes up here swanning round like Tottie Limejuice.'

I was recently emailed by someone who'd come across my pen-name and who told me that there was a music hall character of the early twentieth century who was called Tottie Limejuice. I never had my auntie down as a frequenter of the music halls. She simply would not have had the time, being the eldest girl, always with four or five younger siblings to look after. So either the name was borrowed from her, or she did once manage to sneak away for a night of amusement. I fervently hope it was the latter.

When I took my first tentative steps into the mysterious world of social media, it was largely with promoting the *Sell the Pig* series in mind. So it made sense to open an account in the name of Tottie Limejuice, which I did and used success-fully for about five years.

Recently Facebook decided to have a bit of a purge on any names which they thought were not genuine. The rules are actually strict on what you can or can't call yourself, although I doubt if many of us have actually studied them at length.

I was inclined to agree with them on some points, though. A personal bugbear of mine, and it is only my personal opinion, is tagging the word 'author' on to the end of your name. I don't actually like the word author. It's one of those sounds I dislike. Like lounge. I prefer to call myself a writer, which somehow sounds more workmanlike, at least to my ears.

It also seems a tad pretentious on social media. After all, few other professions add their job title on to their Facebook name, although I have seen those who put their educational degree initials. But I don't see many Fred Smith Plumbers, or Dai Jones Electrician or the like.

So suddenly the Facebook axe started to fall, ruthlessly, and woe betide anyone caught out not using their real name.

The trouble is, this was no 'innocent until proven guilty' policy. If someone, somewhere, decided your Facebook name was not genuine, you were simply locked out of your account until you could prove that it was. The proof requested was in the form of official ID such as a driving licence or credit card. Clearly, I don't have those in my pen-name.

By this time, I already had four books published under the pen-name Tottie Limejuice. But surprisingly enough, someone, somewhere decided it was not a 'real name' and I was locked out of my account until I changed it. It was probably my own fault for being flippant, as usual. I'd joined in a discussion on the subject somewhere and had quipped, 'Oh, how the vicar laughed when he christened me Tottie Limejuice.'

I like being Tottie Limejuice. But it really wasn't worth making a fuss about hanging on to the name. In fact, in a way, it was useful for me and came at the right time. The action came hard on the heels of the publication of my first crime novel, 'Baby's Got Blue Eyes', under the name L M Krier. This unexpected twist gave me the chance to start getting people used to me under another name.

The whole subject of names gets complicated when you try to translate between English and French. And since political correctness now dictates that first names can no longer be called Christian names, which is fine by me, as a Pagan, I get more than a little confused with what to call things.

Surname is easy enough, except for the French, as *surnom* means nickname. Surname to them is just *nom*, name, or *nom de famille*, family name. That's good, and easy enough. Mine is Tither, to rhyme with hither, and it's relatively unusual. It seems to have Irish origins, although before that it may have come from Spain, via the Armada, with a different spelling.

My first name is Lesley, but nobody ever calls me that. To friends and family, although there are few of the latter left these days, I have always been Les. Or, in typical Lancashire fashion, and with that accent, to my Auntie Ethel I was always 'our lickle Les', to which I would always, from being quite small, reply firmly, 'Not little!'

The French are pretty stumped by Tither, with its dreaded, to them, 'th' sound, but Lesley is also a name they are not accustomed to, so they struggle a bit with its spelling and pronunciation. One friend calls me 'Lease-lay', another is convinced I am Lindsey, and it's often written without the second E when people write it for me. But then I did have problems in America where they seemed to want to call me Lessley, rather than the British pronunciation 'Lezley'.

I say British, rather than English, because apparently the name is Scottish in origin and means 'from the grey fortress.' My parents always professed to have no idea why they chose it for me. I did have an uncle with the same name but the British usually make a distinction in the spelling between the sexes. My ex-father-in-law was Leslie, so for a time we had the same first and family names, at least by pronunciation. Women usually use the -ey ending, men normally take the -ie ending, but names are variable, and so is spelling.

Every year there seems to be a fashion, especially among 'celebs' to come up with the weirdest name to inflict on their unfortunate off-spring. It's a long and honourable tradition in the rock world, with such classic examples as Zowie Bowie and Moon Unit Zappa. And there's now a baby girl in the States called Elsie Otter. That's going to go down well when she starts school.

The fashion doesn't seem to have hit France to quite the same degree, yet. Certainly not round here. Although I have heard of one child in the area called Palombe, which is a wood pigeon, which must go down well when she's introducing herself to new potential friends.

I asked my English students about unusual names. Apparently Prune is one, which means Plum. Then there is the usual spattering of hippy-celeb handles like Cheyenne. One student has a young family member called Elaia, which is pretty enough, but it means Skylark in Breton so again, probably poses problems for the child at school.

Back to my names. I have a second first name, if you follow me. On forms now it says middle name but mine isn't my middle name because I have another one before my surname. Even someone as mathematically challenged as I am knows it's difficult to have a middle of four when it comes to names.

I'm not going to tell you my second one as I hate it and never use it, except as an initial. The initial is M and it was inflicted on me by my ultra-religious father, known locally as Holy Joe, as he was forever at church. And my third first name, if you're still following me, is the Luxembourg family name, Krier, which rhymes with queer, not town crier, so you can imagine some of the nicknames I was given growing up.

That gives me a total of four names, and the initials LMKT,

or Elham Katy, as a friend once nicknamed me. The possibilities are endless.

Of all my names and guises, I remain particularly fond of Tottie. But when I started writing crime fiction, I didn't feel she was quite the right fit for the genre. The name has already been mistaken for a porn star on more than one occasion.

Tottie wasn't the only one to fall foul of the real name policy on Facebook. Native Americans, drag queens and transgender people, to name a few, also found their names were deemed 'not real'. It caused quite an outcry. I didn't mind too much but, as with anything else, I didn't like the inequality of it, as for sure, many of the 'celebs' on there were not using the names they were born with.

But meanwhile I had plenty of names to juggle with to come up with pseudonyms for various social media accounts and pen-names for the various different genres I was now writing. Tottie Limejuice would remain my name for the travel memoirs.

For the crime, I quite liked the idea of using initials, rather than a first name. I know some readers aren't keen on crime written by women, despite some of the best of the crime writers over the years having been women. It's not always easy for a writer to capture just the right voice when writing in the personality of the opposite sex. I've read some really cringe-worthy attempts, but also some excellent stuff. I decided to play safe by calling myself L M Krier for the crime books.

I was about to embark on yet another writing adventure – my first children's book. I was going to need a completely different pen-name for that, as clearly the crime one would be unsuitable and Tottie, bless her, might be a bit suggestive for younger readers. Or at least for their parents and grandparents, who would be buying the book for them.

I'd written a full-length children's book about a pony many years ago, when I ran my holiday riding centre in Wales, and never done anything with it. It was long before the days of word processors or computers so it had all been carefully typed out then had sat, forgotten, in a cardboard box, through many house moves.

When I was living in Lincolnshire, I suddenly felt the urge to write another. Most of what I write is loosely based on events, people and characters I've happened on in my own life. So when I decided to write a children's adventure story involving a dog, it was not surprising that I based the canine character on my lovely old border collie, Meic, who moved to France with me.

'The Dog with the Golden Eyes' had been written in a more technologically advanced age than the pony tale, so that had sat on an old floppy disc for many years, gathering dust and cobwebs. When I thought I ought to pull it out, dust it off and see if it was worth resurrecting, I was almost thwarted as I no longer had anything which could read a floppy of that size.

Enter a good friend, Sara, who still lives in Lincolnshire, and is a techie wizard. She kindly sent me a clever device which could be plugged into my laptop, read the disc, and save its contents on to my modern laptop. I wouldn't even have known what to start hunting for on Google.

I'm my own worst critic. I tend never to be satisfied with what I write, which I think is preferable to becoming complacent. But I was reasonably pleased with 'Golden Eyes', and with a few tweaks to modernise it slightly, I thought it was just about worthy of seeing the light of day.

I sent it out to my beta readers, that trusty band of second eyes who look over everything I write to make sure it makes a degree of sense. They agreed, but were all unanimous on one thing. It needed illustrations to bring it to life.

Facebook is the most marvellous place for meeting people. It's incredible how well networking works on social media. I discovered a brilliant illustrator who was ready, willing and able to work on 'Golden Eyes' for me. With any luck, it should be out around the time you are reading this and who knows, it may even be topping the charts.

I delved into my name arsenal and came up with L M Kay for children's books. Short, sweet and simple, and pretty much my own names.

Dear old Tottie had another sortie before 'Golden Eyes' hit the shelves and Kindles of the nation. I was approached by someone I know through Facebook to contribute a chapter to a book being sold for research into Alzheimer's disease. My mother had a different type of dementia, but it's a cause I'm happy to support. Eight writers in total added a bit each to the story, a couple of illustrators brought the work to life and I came up with the title and collective pen-name.

For my joint project with Doris Bird and Farmer Bird, it had been simple enough to borrow a bit from each of our names to create Jilli Lime-Holt. I was asked to come up with something similar for the little charity book, which was a children's story about a cat. Blending eight names seamlessly proved beyond me so the book, Little Kitty the Cat Burglar, went out under the pen-name of Caterina Longtail.

That's twice now I've dabbled in 'team writing'. It's not my strong point. I've never been a team player, always too much of an individual. I'd never say never, especially in writing projects, but the two experiences definitely confirmed for me that when it comes to writing, I prefer to go my own way, at my own speed. And of late, I prefer to do it in the company of DI Ted Darling.

Chapter Twenty-five
Vive la Différence!

Although I have chosen to take French nationality, I recognise that I will never, truly, become a French person, even if I ever become fluent in the language and the body language. There is just too big a gulf between the French and the Anglo-Saxon part of my genetic make-up.

One thing which often separates nations, no matter how cosmopolitan we become through the world-shrinking Internet, is the sense of humour. On Facebook, I am constantly at pains to add smileys to my frequent tongue in cheek comments in the hopes of preventing them from being misunderstood. Of course, there are those who don't seem to understand what the various emoticons mean either, so they still get their knickers in a twist about what I post. But at least I try.

When I first visited France on that memorable school exchange trip in the sixties, our pen-friends took my friend Meg and me to the cinema to see a comedy film. Part of it was supposed to show Scotland Yard and had all the police officers running round in kilts. Our pen-friends couldn't understand why Meg and I were not howling with laughter as they were.

Even in the same nation, humour is a truly individual thing. When I was in digs in the north of England, whilst learning to be a journalist at college in Preston, that ground-breaking alternative comedy programme, Monty Python's Flying Circus, had recently started being shown on television. I remember my landlady sitting gazing at it in utter bewilderment for quite some time before saying, 'This isn't a circus.'

I call it the Marmite effect. The fact that some people can find a certain thing side-splittingly hilarious whilst at the same time it leaves others cold. For me, Marmite is most definitely the by-product of the devil's bowels, while my best friend Jill loves it so much she has been known to take a jar with us on our trail-riding adventures abroad. Mind you, this is the same person I once saw make herself a cheese, peanut butter and lettuce sandwich – and eat it.

The most striking difference in humour which I've noticed since living here is how much more earthy French humour is than British. Well, that's not strictly true. It's more a case of them not having this strange 'watershed' notion which the British have. That if rude words and vulgar innuendo are restricted to after nine o'clock in the evening, they will somehow avoid corrupting the young or shocking the sensibilities of anyone delicate. It's probably partly because French children seem to stay up quite late, at least in my experience, so the watershed would not protect them.

I like to listen to *France Bleu Pays d'Auvergne* radio station, which is rather like one of the BBC regional channels in the UK. It's a mix of music, news, quizzes and magazines. Nothing too heavy, great for improving vocabulary and finding out more about my area. Just before four-thirty in the afternoons is a slot called *La Blague à Lolo,* Lolo being an abbreviation for the first name Laurent, as it's presented by Laurent Boucry. So, Lolo's Joke, a sort of joke of the day slot.

Of course, with text-speak becoming increasingly international, there's another little play on words there with LOL being used for Laugh Out Loud and not, as David Cameron once famously claimed to believe, for Lots of Love.

In that afternoon slot I have heard jokes which run the full gamut of dubious taste subjects, including the female orgasm, premature ejaculation and erectile dysfunction. And I hasten to remind you here that I am a former journalist who has worked in an all-male newspaper office. There is not a swear word I haven't heard, repeatedly, in my life. But even I was stunned, at that time of day, to hear the one about the nun and the banana.

Another thing I've noticed about the French is that they tend not to be as candid and open in talking about themselves as the British are. British friends who run language holidays told me they had some young women come to stay at their house for an English course. It wasn't until almost the end of their visit that one of them mentioned in passing that she already knew the house, as it had belonged to her grandparents before my friends bought it. A Brit would probably have been bursting to share that nugget as soon as they got through the door. Or maybe even on their booking form.

A French friend told me that no French person would write in the soul-baring style of the *Sell the Pig* books. It made me worry a little as to whether there would be a market for a French translation. It seems there definitely is, simply because it is so different to what is available here. There's a degree of the *voyeur* in most of us, so reading all the nitty-gritty of someone else's life may well seem shocking but it does still have a degree of compulsion.

I'm writing this chapter at the end of October, so we are coming up to an important French tradition, which is not at all the same in Britain - November 1st, All Saints Day. It's when the French visit the graveyards to put flowers on family graves, especially chrysanthemums. For weeks leading up to *Toussaint*, All Saints, the markets are full of tubs of the plants.

Our small market in Olliergues is held on the cobbled square in front of the *mairie*, town hall, which now houses our wonderful library on the ground floor. Historically, it was a market hall, an important centre for the hemp trade. Honestly, what are you like? Not that sort of hemp, this wasn't the Stoner capital of France! This was hemp for making canvas, especially for making sailcloth formerly used by the French navy.

Once all the flowers are spread out on the square, it's a magnificent autumnal sight. Each pot is a dense clump of blossoms in purples, yellows, burnt oranges, burgundies. It's never been a flower I'm particularly fond of but I still find it rather sad that all those bright colours are doomed to end their days sitting wilting on a grave. Chrysanths are one of the few flowers still reliably blooming at this time of year so are the obvious choice for the *Toussaint* tradition.

Another thing I've noticed is that the French in general tend to have a phobia about *sucré, salé* cooking, the mix of sweet and savoury on the same plate. It's something the British tend to grow up with, mint jelly with lamb, apple sauce with pork, pineapple with gammon. I've just eaten duckling with a lime marmalade glaze prior to writing this chapter. Most of my French friends throw up their hands in horror at the mere suggestion.

One of my former students, asked to list what she thought were the differences between the two nations, said, 'The English eat green jelly with their meat.'

I always enjoyed watching *Un Dîner Presque Parfait,* France's version of the British TV show, Come Dine with Me. In it, total strangers took turns to cook dinner for each other, then awarded marks. The criticism in the French version was savage and unrestrained, often being dished out during the meal itself. Nothing was more likely to make sparks fly than serving a *sucré, salé* dish to complete strangers. Strange, for a country with lots of Thai cuisine.

Trying to make arrangements to meet my brother for coffee tomorrow reminds me of something else that the Brits find inexplicable about the way the French do things. I'm off to a spa to soak my aching muscles in warm, bubbling volcanic water and sweat out impurities in the hammam. Although not much of a swimmer, I will enjoy a few hesitant laps of both indoor and outdoor pools, because they're there.

It's a big and a popular place, with beauty treatments,

massage, a sauna and all sorts of other delights as well as the swimming pools. But there's no café. All there is by way of refreshment is a vending machine with chocolate bars and bottled water. In Britain there would doubtless be a whole-food health bar selling fresh fruit and veggie smoothies, or 'smoozees' as the French call them, and all kinds of trendy super-food salads and snacks, with lots of quinoa and chickpeas.

It's the same with garden centres here. I've not yet found one which has a café as so many in Britain do. It used to be a favourite outing with my mother, a garden centre with tea and cake after shopping. Although it is now becoming more the thing for the *boulangeries* (bread shops) to have a few tables and to offer tea and coffee, sometimes even breakfast or a snack lunch.

One thing I do notice is that a lot of French people chew gum, something I never consciously remarked in the UK. A lot of them do it with their mouths open, too.

I thought it might be fun to ask French friends what they see as the most striking differences between the English and the French. I did a straw poll of the students I had been teaching at the workshops in Olliergues. Their answers were interesting, to say the least.

Inevitably, my good friend and class comedian, Domi, in response to my question, 'What do you think is different between the French and the English,' quickly quipped, 'You speak well English.'

The students were unanimous in their belief that all British people eat a full English breakfast, every day. I couldn't tell you the last time I ate one. Probably twenty-five years ago when I was once again in digs, studying for an Advanced National Certificate in Equine Business management, affectionately known as an Anceybum.

There was nearly an international incident over the subject of politeness. We were having this conversation after Avril took my group over, so there were two Brits and four French people in the conversation. The French were adamant that the English are more polite. Avril and I were equally adamant that they are not.

We tried to explain how delightful we find it to be greeted with a 'bonjour, madame' wherever we go and how no one would ever greet us with 'good morning, madam' in England, unless they were a salesperson after our money. Nor that you would never see teenage boys greeting one another with a handshake as they do outside schools and colleges here. We had to agree to differ.

Once again the subject of different humour came up, with all four of the students saying they could not understand Mr Bean and his popularity. I thought that rich from a country which still frequently shows repeats of that most politically incorrect of all British comedians, Benny Hill, chasing scantily-clad young women in speeded up films.

Chapter Twenty-six
So Long, Farewell …

As the song from the *Sound of Music goes*. The time has come for the parting of the ways. I hope you've enjoyed my company as much as I've enjoyed yours. But there can be no more *Sell the Pig*. I am too settled in my ways now. I doubt my life has any vast sea changes ahead and to keep on churning out more of the same would not be fair to you, my valued readers.

These days, every man and his dog, literally, write their memoirs. Some of them just can't resist writing one more volume. And then one more. I'm sure we've all known the disappointment of a much-loved television programme which is strung out for just one more series, with disastrous results. The same happens with books, and films. Don't even get me started on the second Marigold Hotel film.

The temptation with memoirs is often to start exaggerating the characters until they become like a caricature. I try to avoid that. It's my personal view that it you have to resort to that to raise a smile, the character was probably not that funny to start with. But that's just my opinion.

I certainly have no intention of stopping writing. It's not within my conscious control to do so. At least not as long as the arthritic fingers can still whiz about on the keyboard and the few remaining little grey cells can still string together a sentence. I will continue to write. Just the subject matter will be different.

A few people have said I should write a prequel to the *Sell the Pig* series, especially about the eight years I owned and ran a holiday riding centre a thousand feet up a wind-swept Welsh mountain, often looking after twenty horses on my own. There's definitely some scope there for a few tales, both funny and sad.

I certainly want to write more crime. In fact DI Ted Darling is insistent that I should do so, and keeps invading my dreams with that intention.

But unless something completely unforeseen happens to change my life beyond recognition, this is where the *Sell the Pig* series ends.

If you are able to follow me on Facebook via the Tottie Limejuice Chat Group, you'll have seen the frequent photos of my grottage, my dogs and the surrounding area which I post on there. If not, let me paint you a little pen-portrait so you can imagine it all more clearly.

My now cosy but still not fully finished grottage sits back to back with the neighbouring house, at right-angles to a quiet road, from which it is set back. It's a classic three up, two down house. The hand-made half-glazed oak stable door opens directly into a traditional kitchen, large enough to accommodate the table on which I work away at my computer. I spend a lot of time there.

Whenever the weather allows, the door is wide open and Fleur and Rosie can come and go as they please while I'm working. I've mentioned never wearing make-up and attacking my own hair with the clippers. Add to that my sartorial style, which is definitely teenage tomboy. A fleece or hoody, jeans and boots for cold weather, crops, a polo and sandals when it's hot. Don't own a single dress or skirt, haven't worn one since the eighties. And there's nothing in my wardrobe that didn't come from a *vide grenier* (attic sale) or drastically reduced in a shop sale.

Outside the door – there is only one, as the house is back to back, yet I tend always to call it the back door – is a large decked area where I like to sit to eat whenever possible. There's a decent sized garden with grass, too churned up by playful dog paws to be properly called a lawn, with a herbaceous border opposite the house and roses and shrubs on two other sides. The fence at the bottom of the garden is buried beneath blackberry bushes, so I only have to stroll a few yards to pick a bowlful for my supper, once they are ripe.

Beyond that fence is what you might call the deal-breaker for the house. The view alone is worth twice what I paid for the property. Due west lies the *chaîne des Puys*, the volcanic chain, with almost a hundred volcanoes. I can't see all of them but the Puy de Dôme itself is prominently visible. At the right time of year, the sun sets directly behind it and the colours are spectacular.

The middle distance boasts a ruined castle on top of another volcanic puy. Coming closer are rolling wooded hills, spectacular always in autumn as the leaves turn, with open fields in between, dotted with cattle, often the glorious mahogany red Salers breed.

At the bottom of the field beyond my boundary fence is an allotment shed with a tin roof. It's a favourite place for Bibi, my little black and white cat, to go and soak up the stored warmth of the sun. Literary pun alert – a cat on a hot tin roof. She's a funny little cat, slightly better trained at recall than the dogs. I call her name and she comes galloping up the field, hurdling the fences as she comes, like an extra from Lassie Come Home.

Poor little Bibi had a nasty accident one evening while doing her thing. I was calling her and wondering why she didn't appear, which was unlike her, so I went to take a look. I didn't consciously see her at first, then realised she was hanging upside down from the top of the fence, part way down the field, seemingly trapped by a back leg.

It was only a couple of days since I'd lost Ci so I was in a fragile frame of mind. I ran to the gate of the field then went pelting as fast as I could to find out what had happened. In jumping over the fence, she had clearly caught a back foot in the top strand of wire which, as she fell, had twisted round, trapping her foot.

I managed to release her, with a bit of pulling and panting, but she couldn't bear any weight on the leg, so I picked her up and rushed her off to the vet. Fortunately, my own lovely vet was back from his holidays so we went there, as fast as I could drive without risking a speeding fine.

Luckily, there was no serious damage. She clearly hadn't been stuck for all that long, thank goodness, and her foot and leg had just gone to sleep from being compressed by the wire. A quick injection and some anti-inflammatory tablets and all would be well.

It was the first time I had seen my own vet since losing Ci, although I had phoned him to tell him what had happened, as he had kindly responded to my attempts to contact him by leaving a message asking if there was anything he could do.

I've heard Brits moving out to France expressing concern that they wouldn't be able to find a vet who would care as much about their pets as their vet in England had done. I've even heard disgruntled ex-pats in France claim that this is, in fact, the case. All I can say is, from my experience, vets here are every bit at good, and as kind, compassionate and considerate, as any of their counterparts in Britain.

When I asked lovely Dr Girardin if it could have been my fault that Ci had died so suddenly, because I had perhaps not acted quickly enough at the first sign of something wrong, then promptly burst into tears, he was kindness itself. He explained that from what I told him of the symptoms and diagnosis, there was nothing more than could have been done. And he waved away all apology about my emotional outburst.

Sadly he has now retired and moved away. He was a lovely man and an excellent diagnostician. I now take both dogs and cats to the smart, new, fully-equipped veterinary clinic in the same town, where there are good vets. But I miss our old vet, who was so kind, patient and gentle with Ci in particular. He never seemed busy, always had time for a long chat. We had some lively and interesting debates on a wide range of topics, such as why England felt it necessary to slaughter badgers rather than vaccinate cattle to get TB under control. I will miss him.

I finally managed to get my pension status sorted out and to be re-issued with my magic *carte vitale*. Of course, in typical French fashion, when I got the card, my doctor was on strike. The French are big on striking, and most professions do it. As a former Trades Unionist myself, I support their right to do so. It's better than moaning and doing nothing.

So life for me goes on pleasantly in my little corner of France. As for describing the stunning wild countryside of the Auvergne in a way to bring it to life for you, that is beyond even my capabilities as a professional wordsmith. You'll simply have to come and see for yourself. Tottie's Tours will no doubt supply me with enough unique material for at least one more book. Perhaps you will be one of the stars of the story.

Until then, so long, farewell, auf Wiedersehen, adieu.

And finally, in honour of my mother …

The End.

More From The Same Author

Writing as L M Krier
Baby's Got Blue Eyes

Chapter One
introducing DI Ted Darling

Ted Darling snapped out an arm to stifle the strident ring of the mobile phone on the bedside table before it woke his sleeping partner. At the same time he smiled to himself at the absurdity of the gesture.

As he took the call, he looked over his shoulder to where Trevor lay spread-eagled between the tousled sheets. Trevor always slept like a starfish, a dead one at that, taking up an incredible amount of space for such a slim, lithe figure.

Ted was reduced to a few meagre inches at the very edge of the bed, with one arm and leg hanging out. What little room

Trev was not taking up was occupied by an assortment of cats, seven, if they were all there as usual.

Trev was still sleeping the deep sleep of the innocent, silky-black curls framing a head-turning face. Outrageously long, thick black lashes to the lids concealed those devastating baby blue eyes which meant Trev was seldom refused anything.

'Hello?' growled Ted quietly. He had long since given up answering the phone using his surname – it took too long dealing with the inevitable wisecracks of his gruff voice opening the conversation with 'Darling'.

He listened, grunting a few times, then said: 'Shit. I'm on my way.'

The discovery of a body meant there was no time for a shower if Ted wanted to get there ahead of the circus, which was always his preference. He'd have to make do with a quick squirt of deodorant, a bit of mouthwash and finger combing his hair.

Ted was, as they say, small yet perfectly formed. So small that people seldom believed him when he told them he was a copper, despite the minimum height requirement having long since gone. He was in such good shape he would pass for ten years younger than his forty. Trev largely saw to that, along with the sports Ted packed into whatever free time he had. There was not an ounce of fat anywhere on his body, just hard, defined muscle.

His hair was the sort of thick dirty blonde which would probably never thin nor go grey. His eye colour would have artists and interior designers arguing for hours. Light hazel, tending to muddy green, depending on his prevailing mood.

He slipped on dark jeans, added a cotton polo, picked up his leather jacket and headed for the garage, car keys already in hand. The early morning was still cold and things were quiet in the cul-de-sac of modest semis on an estate which had been reasonably respectable when he and Trev had set up home there ten years ago.

Nowadays Ted tended to know more of his neighbours through his work than through any social life, although he largely kept to himself and left uniform to deal with the antics of the local scallies. The extra locks on the garage were not for his elderly but reliable Renault but to protect Trev's baby, a shiny Triumph Bonneville T100, with its red custom paint, largely paid for by Ted.

It was not far from the house to the location of the body, not even far enough for the Renault's heater to make any difference to the chilly interior. Ted swung off Marple Road and continued down a no through road towards playing fields at the bottom. He spotted a squad car on blues, parked across the road at the end, and two PCs starting to unwind tape to protect the crime scene.

Ted pulled up, lowered his window, and greeted the two men with a 'Morning, what we got?'

'Morning sir,' one of them replied. 'She's across the far side of the fields, down the bank towards the river. A couple of your team are there already and the doc's just arrived.'

Ted gave them a thanks, then pulled out a packet of Fisherman's Friend sweets from his jacket pocket. He waved them at the nearest of the PCs and asked: 'How many for this one?'

'You'll probably get away with one for this one, sir, she's fresh!' he called back cheerfully, pulling the tape back so the DI could drive through.

Everyone had their own way of dealing with the gruesome side of the job. Ted's was his addiction to the strong menthol sweets he always kept in his pocket. It was a standing joke at the nick, how many the DI would need to munch his way through for the worst of the bodies.

Ted followed a tarmac road round to the far side of the playing fields, where the vehicles parked told him that most of the Scenes of Crime and allied services had just arrived and were going about their business. A passing officer directed him over to the trees where he could see others making their way down a narrow path.

It was almost fully daylight now but it would be darker in the woods, especially underfoot, so Ted had taken his Maglite from the glove compartment before he headed in the same direction. The short path led down to the riverbank, opening out into a wide grassy space. Ted saw that two of his team were already on site.

DCs Tina Bailey and Rob O'Connell were good solid officers, so he knew the basic groundwork would be done faultlessly. He heard the police surgeon before he saw him. Tim Elliott seemed to have a perpetual cold or a succession of allergies. If it was true that sneezing destroyed brain cells, it was a wonder he was still functioning at all, let alone as a doctor.

In his usual way the doctor started speaking even before Ted had reached him, with no sign of a greeting, just plunging straight in with whatever chaotic thoughts were circulating through his brain.

'Definitely dead, definitely not natural causes, throat's been cut cleanly. Been dead anything up to forty-eight hours, I would say. Not killed here, killed elsewhere and brought here. Both breasts have been removed with what looks like surgical precision.

'Bizarrely, on first examination, it looks as if all her body hair has been removed very recently, possibly after death, and the body may have been cleaned in some way. Her head is shaved, pubic hair is missing, none anywhere else on the body. Going to be an interesting one.'

He was already walking away before he'd finished the last sentence, so Ted threw a 'goodbye' at his retreating back and turned back to his DCs.

'Fill me in,' he said.

'The guy over there found her, sir,' Rob said. 'Luckily he had the presence of mind to back away before he chucked his breakfast up, so the crime scene is relatively uncontaminated.'

Ted threw a glance towards the man. 'What was he doing down here at that time of the morning?' he asked.

'Walking his dog, sir,' Rob replied. 'The German Shepherd attached to him by a lead is a bit of a giveaway.'

Rob knew he could get away with the odd wisecrack with the DI, who was the best he had ever served under. There was a line he knew it was unwise to cross, but he hoped that he had stayed on the right side of it, despite the look the DI threw at him.

'Must have been dark when he found her though. Bit of an odd time for a dog walk?'

'Have you seen the size of that dog, boss?' Rob answered. 'I wouldn't be worried walking anywhere at any time of day or night with that brute next to me.'

'Fair enough. Legit, do you think?'

'Yes sir, definitely on the level, I would say. He looks really shaken up. I'll give him time to come to a bit before I get a statement from him,' Rob replied.

'Any ID on her? What do we know about her?'

Ted was looking towards the naked body all the time they spoke, munching his Fisherman's Friend, but he made no attempt to approach too close. He left that to the experts.

Tina answered this time. 'No ID anywhere we can see so far, sir, and no sign of a weapon. She was left totally naked, no signs of any clothing or personal possessions in the immediate vicinity. Alice looks to be early twenties from what we can see and from what the doc confirmed.'

Tina always gave a name to any unidentified body until the real ID was discovered. She said it was more personal, a way of humanising the body rather than just referring to it as 'the body' all the time. Ted was in favour of anything to increase respect amongst his officers, so was happy to go along with it.

'Right, thorough ground work here, witness statement from the dog walker, knock on some doors on your way back. Quite a way to lug a body from the nearest place to park a car. Someone may well have seen or heard something. I'll organise some reinforcements from uniform for a site search.

'We need to find a weapon, clothing, personal effects, anything at all to help us,' Ted told them. 'Let's try and get an ID as soon as we can, so when you get back in get started on checking Missing Persons for a possible match. I'm going in to brief the Boss. We're a team member down and we need someone good on this one, by the look of things.'

He'd just lost possibly the best Detective Sergeant he had ever worked with. When the shakes first started, Jack Gregson probably thought, like the rest of them, that he'd been hitting the bottle harder than he realised. He even went on the wagon for a few months, but it didn't make any difference and his symptoms just kept getting worse.

The diagnosis of Parkinson's disease came right out of left field. It rarely affects people under fifty and Gregson had only just turned forty. It brought his career to an abrupt end and took away Ted's right-hand man and a good one, who would be hard to replace.

Time to turn up the pressure on the DCI to get him the promised replacement. This case looked as if he was going to need his team up to full strength and with the best manpower available to him.

Writing collectively as
Jilli Lime-Holt
Take Three Birds

Chapter One

Hatching an Idea

Facebook – via Private Message

Jilli: I've had a brilliant idea!

Tottie: <groan> Why does that announcement fill me with trepidation?

Jilli: No, really, something that might make us a bit of money.

Tottie: Now you have my attention. What?

Jilli: We could write a book.

Tottie: I think you'll find that's been done, you daft Doris.

Jilli: No, write one between us. The three of us, you, me and Posh Bird. About meeting up on Facebook and really getting on.

Tottie: I think that's probably been done.

Jilli: No, but people who might not have met in real life and then find they really get on and become like best friends. And then, here's the twist, they're from three different countries, then they all meet up in one country.

Tottie: It would have to be France. You know I never leave the Auvergne.

Jilli: Fab! I don't go anywhere either, I get homesick at the end of my drive but I could come to you and Posh could too, we could all meet there.

Tottie: Helluva long way for you to drive on your own though. Why doesn't Posh fly out to you then you both come

179

together? Bit of a road trip on the way, like Thelma and Louise. Just don't drive near any canyons.

Jilli: Then we all write exactly what we think of one another.

Tottie: This could all end in tears.

Jilli: It will be brill! It's not been done before like this.

Tottie: Sort of chick lit meets reality. Chickality? Is that a genre? Bloody good idea, Doris. Well done, Bird.

Jilli: Not such a daft Doris with this idea. I'll ask Posh Bird, hang on ...

five minutes later

Jilli: She's in – we're on!!

a few weeks later ...

Jilli: Posh is out, family stuff.

Tottie: I know, you daft Doris, I was in on the same PM. Shame, but obviously family stuff has to come before friend stuff.

Jilli: Shall we still do it?

Tottie: We need another bird on board. Bit flat with just the two of us. Invent another bird and make it part fiction?

Jilli: I really want to keep it real. We must know another writer who would fit in, from all the writer groups we belong to.

Tottie: Needs to be someone we can trust. Someone who isn't just going to nick the idea and run with it and get a book out before we do.

Jilli: We could sue them for copyright.

Tottie: There's no copyright in an idea, Doris. Who do we know we can trust?

Jilli: We can trust Janet.

Tottie: Which Janet?

Jilli: Janet Farmer

Tottie: Janet as in Farmer Bird Janet? Wowser, good idea,

Bird. We could certainly trust her. Wonder if she'd be up for it?

Jilli: You know her better than I do. Ask her. But does she have a sense of humour?

Tottie: Is the Pope a catholic?

Jilli: Oh yeah, course, I forgot she's from Yorkshire.

Tottie: Don't say that, Bird, you'll start a new War of the Roses!! She's from Derbyshire.

Jilli: Close enough! Ask her, see what she thinks, though is she a young sixty-something like you or an old biddy? I need someone who can share driving to France!

Tottie: Feck, woman, she builds drystone walls for a living!!! She could pick your car up and run with it. But what if we all fall out? She's a farmer so she knows how to use a shotgun!! OK, I'll ask her ...

five minutes later ...

Tottie: I asked her. She's in. She's just ordering her passport. Take Three Birds it is!

Writing as L M Kay
The Dog with the Golden Eyes

Chapter One
The stranger

The most remarkable thing about Nicholas James Corrigan was that he didn't speak. It wasn't that he couldn't speak. The Man he went to see on the first Wednesday afternoon of every month said there was no reason why he should not speak again.

He said the fact that Nicholas James did not even speak in his sleep meant that he was not just putting it on to get attention. He said that one day, when he was ready, he would probably speak again.

Nicholas James used to speak, before the Very Bad Thing happened to him.

Long ago, almost before he could remember, when he was very little, he lived in a nice house. His Mother was there and he thought there was a man as well. They had a big garden, with an apple tree with a swing in it, and a slide for Nicholas James to play on.

Then after that there was a horrible house on an untidy estate and the man was not there any more, just Nicholas James and his Mother.

His Mother was always sad and cried all the time. But sometimes she would laugh a lot and do wild things. Sometimes people came to the house and then she would be happy again for a time.

Then the Very Bad Thing happened and Nicholas James never saw his Mother again, and after that day he did not speak any more.

Nicholas James went to live with his Very Nice Aunt. She lived in a little cottage tucked away up a steep passageway, surprisingly close to all the shops.

The cottage had a tiny garden which was absolutely full of flowers, mostly purple and yellow ones because his Aunt said they attracted more bees and butterflies. Certainly the garden was always full of butterflies, in all sorts of colours and sizes. And birds, which came to feed from the many tables and feeders his Aunt kept filled up for them.

There were tinkling wind chimes hanging from every spare branch in the garden, made of metal and wood and bamboo. They brought the garden alive with their gentle sound. Sometimes the neighbours next door, who were older and liked to complain, would tell the Very Nice Aunt that the wind chimes made so much noise that they could not get to sleep at night. But she just laughed and said there were worse things to have to listen to than wind chimes.

His Aunt adored her garden and loved her plants. The overflow from the garden filled the tiny cottage in an assortment of pots, old kettles and other curious tubs. They were on every windowsill and shelf. Every spare inch where there was room for a plant, there was one.

The Very Nice Aunt did not mind at all that Nicholas James did not speak. She never tried to put pressure on him to speak to her. She called him M*y Silent Hero* and was quite happy for him to write down any messages he wanted to give her.

Because although he did not speak, Nicholas James was an intelligent small boy, and wrote beautifully in a very grown-up italic script on the notepad which he always carried everywhere he went.

His Aunt worked mornings in an office near the shops. Lots of people came in to ask her advice on just about anything, because she was very clever and knew about all sorts of things. In the afternoons she stayed at home and painted, wonderful pictures of her flowers and butterflies and birds. She sold her paintings through a small gift shop, not far from the cottage.

Nicholas James like living with his Aunt. He knew he was lucky, because sometimes small boys with no family had to go and live with aunts who were not very nice. But his was.

He liked the city where they lived. It had a huge, beautiful cathedral right on top of a hill. You could see it for miles around. You always knew, if you had been travelling, that you were nearly home when you could see the lights of the cathedral, up there on the hill.

At first, after the Very Bad Thing, Nicholas James had not gone to school like other small boys of his age. But after a time his Aunt had arranged for him to go to a small private school in an old house, quite near to the cathedral.

Most of the boys at the school sang in the cathedral choir. The music teacher there hoped that one day, when he decided to speak again, Nicholas James would be able to do the same thing. Nicholas James was good at music and could read it well.

Until then the teacher let him sit beside him at the piano, or the organ when they went into the cathedral, and turn the pages while he played. Sometimes at the end of the hymn he would let him play the chord for the Amen, if it was a simple one.

Nicholas James was about as happy as it was possible to be, for a small boy who had seen a Very Bad Thing and whose mother was not there any more. But he was still not happy enough to want to speak.

Nicholas James sighed a lot and sometimes he gave a small weak smile. The friends who came to the cottage to see his Very Nice Aunt did not seem to mind at all that he did not speak. Most of them thought it quite wonderful to meet a polite small boy who did not speak at all.

Nicholas James rather preferred the company of grown-ups because they did not pester him to talk, as the boys at his school sometimes did. They had all been told that they must not, and they must let Nicholas James decide for himself whether or not he wanted to talk. But of course they still did it.

Every Saturday, Nicholas James and his Aunt walked the short distance to the shops for a browse, as she called it. They would buy nice wholesome things to eat from the health food shop, and get fresh fruit and vegetables from a special shop. The Very Nice Aunt did not believe in eating meat or eating things with chemicals on them. Nicholas James didn't mind as he liked the meals his Aunt made for him and there was always plenty to eat.

After they had finished their shopping, the two of them would always go to their favourite book shop for coffee. This was Nicholas James' best treat of the week. He would get a big mug of frothy coffee, made with all milk, and a big piece of cheesecake. If he was lucky he would be able to sit in one of the big squashy armchairs to enjoy them.

The Very Nice Aunt loved books and there were almost as many books in the cottage as there were plants in the garden. Nicholas James had so many books in his tiny bedroom that there was hardly any room for his bed.

One Saturday morning, they were doing their usual round of the shops. As they were climbing up the High Street under the old arch, Nicholas James saw a stray dog. It was a sheepdog, but unusually tall, with long legs. It was very thin and its coat, which was black, white and brown, was dirty and matted.

Although there were people all around it, the dog was just

standing in the middle of the pavement, staring fixedly up at the sky, and occasionally barking quietly to itself. Nicholas James stared hard at the dog but the dog kept right on staring up at the sky, from time to time uttering its strange, quiet little bark.

The Very Nice Aunt commented on how thin the poor dog looked. She loved all animals, although she did not have one because of where she lived and going out to work in the mornings. But the dog just carried on with its strange behaviour, not looking to right or left, although people passing by tried to speak to it.

Nicholas James and his Very Nice Aunt carried on climbing up the High Street. Suddenly Nicholas James became aware that the dog was following them. It was padding along just behind them.

Pad.

Pad.

Pad.

Nicholas James stopped and turned round and looked at the dog, which immediately stopped and again began its strange behaviour, looking up to the sky and barking quietly to itself.

Why do you do that? Nicholas James said, although of course he only said it in his head because he did not speak.

But the dog seemed to have heard and understood what he said because it immediately looked directly at him with sad golden eyes and said, *I do it, Nick Jim, because when I was small a Very Bad Thing happened to me and I haven't seen my mother since. I hope that if I keep looking up to the sky I might see her again.*

And Nicholas James thought that was remarkable, because not only did he understand everything the dog seemed to say to him but also because nobody had ever called him Nick Jim except his Mother. He had not heard himself called that at all since the Very Bad Thing happened.

He also thought is strange that no one had seemed to hear

what the dog had said except him. Certainly his Aunt did not show any signs that she had heard it talking to him.

Nicholas James reached out and took his Very Nice Aunt's hand and tugged gently at it to attract her attention. She immediately turned back to him because she was the sort of grown-up who knew how important it was for small boys not to be ignored when they have something important to show you.

Nicholas James pointed towards the dog, which had gone back to gazing at the sky.

His Aunt said the dog must be a stray and they should perhaps try to contact the RSPCA to see about getting it taken somewhere where it would be safe.

Nicholas James pointed again towards the dog and looked up at his Very Nice Aunt.

She said, 'It wouldn't be fair for us to take him with us because of where we live and not being a really suitable household for a big dog. We could perhaps take him back and give him something to eat while we try to get in touch with the RSPCA. But only if he would like to come with us, because animals must have the freedom to choose, just like we do.'

Nicholas James looked at the dog and the dog looked back at him with its golden eyes. Nicholas James knew that the dog would follow them back to the cottage, so he just turned and started to walk away. The dog padded along behind the two of them.

Pad.

Pad.

Pad.